Alcoholism
A Family Matter

Published by: Health Communications, Inc.
Enterprise Center
3201 Southwest 15th Street
Deerfield Beach, FL 33442

Published by: Health Communications, Inc.
Enterprise Center
3201 Southwest 15th Street
Deerfield Beach, FL 33442

ISBN: 0-932194-24-9

Printed in the United States of America.

TABLE OF CONTENTS

AUTHOR CREDITS

Charles P. Barnard, Ed.D.
Director, Graduate Training Program in Family Therapy
University of Wisconsin—Stout
Menomonie, WI

Mary Bratton, M.S., C.A.C.
Therapist, The Tennyson Center
St. Vincent Medical Center
Toledo, OH

Peter Brown
Adolescent Coordinator
Group Health, Inc.
St. Paul, MN

Andrea Dennison, C.A.C.
Family Treatment Coordinator
ARC/The Terraces
Ephrata, PA

Sharon Wegscheider-Cruse, M.S.W.
President/Director
ONSITE Training & Consulting, Inc.
Palm Desert, CA

H. Stephen Glenn, Ph.D.
President, Family Development Institute
Washington, DC

Terence Gorski, M.A., C.A.C.
President, Alcohol Systems Associates
The CENAPS Corporation
Hazel Crest, IL

Jane Hathaway, B.A., C.A.C.
Family Coordinator
Arms Acres Treatment Center
Scotia, NY

Sandra Cohen-Holmes, M.Ed.
Family Chemical Dependency Consultant
Boston, MA

L. John Key, M.F.C.C.
Co-Director/Co-Founder
Center for Abusive Therapy
Pasadena, CA

Milan Korcok
Contributing Edutor
U.S. Journal of Drug & Alcohol Dependence
Hollywood, FL

Wayne Kritsberg, M.A., C.A.C.
Author, Trainer & Consultant
Private Practitioner
Austin, TX

Merlene Miller, M.A.
Director of Education
Miller Intervention & Recovery Center
Olathe, KS

John O. Neikirk, M.S.
Trainer & Consultant
Private Practitioner
Minneapolis, MN

Eileen M. Oulette, M.D.
Director, University Affiliate Facility
Eunice Kennedy Shriver Center
Waltham, MA

Nancy Whitaker Renaud, M.Ed.
Family Therapist/Trainer
Private Practitioner
Portland, OR

Gerald Shulman, M.A.
Vice President of Clinical Programming
Addiction Recovery Corporation
Waltham, MA

Dene Stamas, M.A., C.A.C.
Director of Alcoholism Programs
Mercy Hospital & Medical Center
Chicago, IL

Sharon Sweeney, Ph.D.
Clinical Psychologist/Co-Director
Center for Abusive Therapy
Pasadena, CA

The Family Tree: Using the Past To Understand and Direct Your Future

By Wayne Kritsberg

People who grow up in alcoholic families generally have a distorted sense of what their family was like and have little information about their family history. Developing a "family tree" can being a sense of clarity and order into what is generally a diffused and muddled memory.

The family tree gives an overview of the family. It is simple to do and easy to read. When it is done correctly, it allows the person who is doing the fmaily tree to see his/her whole family structure on one sheet of paper. S/he can see the relationships between generations, and sometimes, for the first time, be able to trace the disease of alcoholism back through their family history.

Time and again, at workshops with people who are from alcoholic families, and with individual clients who are adult children from alcoholic families, I have heard the following comments:

"I never realized how many alcoholics I have in my family."

"I am amazed at how much I don't know about my family history."

"Seeing my family tree really highlights how alcoholism

has been passed down from generation to generation."

In this article, you, the reader, will be given the opportunity to chart your own family tree. It is hoped that by doing this you will gain some insights and information into your family of origin and that the experience of doing your own family tree will enable you to better teach your clients how to develop their own family trees.

Remember that when developing this type of family tree, use your family of origin rather than the present nuclear family that you may currently be living in (i.e., your wife or husband and your children). We are diagramming your original family (i.e., your mother, father, brothers, sisters, etc.).

The first step is to have a chart that you can use to diagram your family tree. Turn the chart following this article sideways in order to use. The horizontal lines have been numbered. As we proceed with the instructions, the line that we will be working on will be identified with the corresponding number. When you are putting names on the numbered lines, use the first name, middle initial, and last name. When entering women's names on the chart, use their maiden names. This makes it much easier to trace blood lines and lineage.

Line #1. Place your own name on this line. Directly below your name, in the blank unlined space, list the names of **your** brothers and sisters.

Line #2. Place your father's name on this line (remember to use his first name, middle initial, and last name). Directly below his name (in the blank space) list **his** brothers and sisters. That would be your uncles and aunts on your father's side.

3. Line #3. Place your mother's name on this line (remember to always use the maiden name for females). Directly below your mother's name (in the blank space) list **her** brothers and sisters. That would be **your** uncles and aunts on your mother's side.

Line #4. Place your father's father's name on this line (your paternal grandfather). In the space below, list your grandfather's brothers and sisters.

Line #5. Place your father's mother's name on this line (your paternal grandmother). In the space below her name list your grandmother's brothers and sisters.

Line #6. Place your mother's father's name on this line (your maternal grandfather). List your maternal grandfather's brothers and sisters below his name.

Line #7. Place your mother's mother's name on this line (your maternal grandmother). List her brothers and sisters below her name.

Lines #8 & #9. Place the names of your paternal grandfather's father (line #8) and your paternal grandfather's mother (line #9). List brothers and sisters under the appropriate name.

Lines #10 & #11. Place the names of your paternal grandmother's father (line #10) and your paternal grandmother's mother (line #11). List brothers and sisters under the appropriate name.

Lines #12 and #13. Place the names of your maternal grandfather's father (line #12) and your maternal grandfather's mother (line #13). List brothers and sisters under the appropriate name.

Lines #14 and #15. Place the names of your maternal grandmother's father (line #14), and your maternal grandmother's mother (line #15). List brothers and sisters under the appropriate name.

Do not be discouraged if there are places on your family tree that you cannot fill in. Most of us become a little hazy when we try to remember what the names of our grandparents and great-grandparents were. The names of their brothers and sisters are beyond most of us. It is important, however, to try to get the information that will fill in the blanks on the family tree. The family tree can give us an overview of our family and a sense that we belong to a family system.

After the family tree has been completed, review it, look at all of the names that you have filled in, and try to get a sene that each of the names represents a person ... a person who was vital to your history. Remembering stories that you may have heard about different family members will give you a feel for the richness of your family.

At this point, place an "A" next to the name of any person on your chart who either is or was an alcoholic, or who may have had a "drinking problem." It is important to remember that in family oral histories "great uncle Joe" will be remembered as drinking "a bit too much" rather than as an alcoholic. Next, place a "C" next to any family member who may have had cancer.

Coding the names in the above manner can be very enlightening. Most people who do this exercise are amazed to see, graphically displayed, that alcoholism is indeed a disease that "runs in families." Although may people know this itellectually, they don't feel it emotionally until they see it in black and white, written on their family tree.

I ask people to put a "C" next to those family members who have had or hve died from cancer, because cancer seems to be the disease of the co-dependent. I have worked with many people from alcoholic families who, when they do their family tree, find that a vast majority of their family members have either died of alcoholism or of cancer.

Feel free to make up your own code for any other diseases that you may wish to track through your family. Keep in mind, however, that it is the simplicity of the family tree chart that makes it effective. Try not to clutter it up too much.

The person who grows up in an alcoholic family loses much of the memory of their childhood; they also lose a sense of belonging to a larger family system. Developing the family tree can be the first step in the process of filling in the memory loss and emotionally becoming reintegrated into that larger family system. With the awareness of his or her roots, the adult child from an alcoholic family can use the foundations of the past to make changes in the present, so that the future will be healthier and fuller.

Alcoholism & Incest in the Family—Part I: Similar Traits, Common Dynamics

By Charles P. Barnard

One of the earliest pieces of research in the area of incest (Marcuse, 1923), identified chronic alcoholism, or a drunken episode at the least, as a primary variable in the incestuous family. Since that early work, many others have established the connection between alcoholism and incest (Herman, 1981; Nedoma, Mellan, and Pondelickova, 1969; Magal and Winnick, 1968; Tormes, 1968; Machotka, 1967; Cavallin, 1966; Cromier, 1963; Hersko, 1961). The figures range from 15% of incest perpetrators, to as high as 75-80% of all perpetrators in a particular study group (Meiselman, 1978, and Cabinis and Phillip, 1969).

My clinical experience has also documented the existence of a connection between alcoholism and incest. While it would be unrealistic to assert that all families with an adult alcoholic will be found to be incestuous, or that all incestuous families will have an alcoholic adult, clinical experience does suggest that these two behaviors will be found to co-exist considerably beyond the prevalence that would be expected by chance alone. Justice and Justice (1979) have identified alcoholism as one of the six problems they typically need to address with incestuous families.

Lustig and his colleagues (1966) have stated the following, in reference to incest in the family: "If a behavior pattern such as this (incest) reduces family tension and thus contributes to family homeostasis, it tends to become a part of that homeostasis which, once established, tends to be self-perpetuating." While this is certainly true of incest as a regulator of a family's state of equilibrium, the same is true for alcoholism. Three recent books (Barnard, 1981; Stanton, 1982; and Wegscheider, 1981), as well as many articles, have firmly established this. Both incest and alcoholism have the inherent capacity to become a primary stabilizing factor in the life of a family. Much like the outrigger of a South Pacific canoe stabilizes and prevents the canoe from tipping, so does alcoholism/incest stabilize the family and prevent it from "tipping," and ultimate destruction.

As professionals are trained and develop specific areas of diagnostic and treatment expertise, it is those very areas of expertise which will dictate what they most quickly diagnose and treat. Thus, the alcoholism and drug counselor will diagnose and treat drug dependency most readily, while clinicians familiar with incest will quickly diagnose and treat that behavior. It seems that as professionals, we diagnose and treat that which we know best how to diagnose and treat. Once the similarities are brought into our consciousness or diagnostic awareness, hopefully both phenomena can be appropriately diagnosed and treatment efforts implemented.

This article will identify similarities between "alcoholic" and "incestuous" families. The similarities seem fairly blatant, but as blatant as they are, it is unfortunate how often the alcoholism will be observed and treated, but the incest overlooked, or vice versa. One study has identified the likelihood of over 90% of incest cases never coming to the attention of any social agency (Gagnon, 1965). The inherent problem in treating one of these problems, but not the other, is that the potential for preventing recidivism is diminished.

Similarities of Alcoholic and Incestuous Families

The following comprises a representative identification of similarities between these two family problems. For purposes of this article, family. broad and generic characteristics are identified as opposed to more micro-characteristics.

- **Blurred generational boundaries.** As Justice and Justice

(1979), among others, have identified the blurring of generational boundaries as characteristic of the incestuous family, Barnard (1981) and Stanton (1982) have identified generational blurring as also typical of the alcoholic family. As the adult/marital relationship deteriorates, there is an increased likelihood of one of the children being "selected" to fill the role of surrogate spouse. Naturally, this can easily culminate in an incestuous relationship, and even if this is not the final outcome, this type of maneuver has detrimental effects on both the developing child and the total family operation. The blurring of these generational boundaries is what Haley (1976) and Minuchin (1974) have identified as being inevitably linked to the development of human problems.

- **Dysfunctional marital dyad, with a fragmented to non-existent parental dyad.** In both of these types of families, there is a problematic marital and parental dyad. Just as the existence of this phenomena can lead to the blurred generational boundaries identified above, it is similarly destructive to the total family operation. Lewis and colleagues (1976), along with Satir (1964), among others, have identified how the two adults are the "architects of the family." If their relationship is dysfunctional, there is a heightened probability that the entire family will also be troubled. The absence of a strong marital/parental relationship increases the likelihood that one of the children will become "parentified" and elevated to the status of a "pretend spouse," at least emotionally, if not sexually.

- **Deterioration of the marital sexual relationship.** As the sexual relationship between the two adults deteriorates, the probability that incest will occur is increased. Strack and Dutton (1971), have reported that nearly 100% of all married alcoholics report sexual dysfunctions in their marriages. As diminished sexual contact between mother and father progress, and the debilitating effect of alcohol on one's moral consciousness occurs, the probability of incest must be considered. Similarly, the guilt and shame attached to incestuous behavior can serve to stimulate an even greater need for the numbing effect of alcohol.

- **Normal inhibitory anxieties are short-circuited or muted**. Both family types will experience the inhibition of normal anxieties which otherwise monitor the development of incestuous relationships in the family. Alcohol, as is well known, acts upon the brain in such a fashion that normal inhibitory regulators are short-circuited. Similarly, in the incestuous family, normal inhibitory anxieties are muted, if not by alcohol, then through the utilization of repressive defense mechanisms. In either case, the outcome is an increased likelihood of the incestuous boundary being violated and the alcoholism and incest forming a vicious cycle.

- **Family affect is muffled and distorted.** If one considers each individual, and family, as having an "emotional keyboard," the individuals in these families only have a few keys available for "free play." These families will have difficulty with open expression of either aggression, or affection, or both. It is as though these families perceive themselves as too fragile and brittle to allow expression of aggression without disintegration, or too feeble and weak to express and receive affection, out of fear of being absorbed and losing what little sense of self they do retain.

- **Denial is rampant and "secrets" predominate.** As denial has been identified as a hallmark characteristic of the alcoholic (Jellinek, 1960), and alcoholic family (Jackson, 1954; and Wegscheider, 1981), so is the same true of the incestuous family. Both family operations utilize inordinate amounts of psychic energy to maintain the "secrets" which deprive them of the potential for greater emotional expression and relatedness. As destructive as the maintenance of the secret obviously is, it is perceived by all involved as being important to preserve and maintain the delicately fragile equilibrium of the family. The activation of denial serves to further "enable" the alcoholism and incest since confrontation and intervention are avoided.

- **Family roles are pathologically assigned and calcified.** As individuals are rigidly assigned roles in the alcoholic family (Barnard, 1981; Black, 1981; Wegscheider, 1981; Stanton, 1982), the same type of calcification, and resultant problems, are observed in the incestuous family. In these families there is pathological assignment of roles, with children rigidly functioning in adult roles and adults frequently appearing helpless and in need of guidance, as is expected of children.

- **The family becomes isolated, emotionally and otherwise**. The alcoholic family isolates itself through the mechanisms of denial and erroneous problem-solving. So, too, does the incestuous family isolate itself. Lutier (1961) has even gone so far as to suggest that isolation is the major variable associated with the evolution of incestuous relationships. The family closes itself off to outside involvement and stimulation, and begins to engage in the process of "self suffocation." Justice and Justice have said: "One final effect of the family while incest is going on is that the father's dependence on his daughter leads, as we noted, to his being jealous and overpossessive. His behavior interferes with her making normal social contacts, and the whole family becomes increasingly isolated."

As these families effectively cut themselves off from outside involvement, they further seal their fate by insuring the continuation of the alcoholic and incestuous cycles. In this way, the alcoholism/incest comes to both a cause and effect of the overall family organization and operation.

• **A profound state of pathologically rigid homeostasis or "stuckness."** The maneuvers which these families use to adapt to the incest/alcoholism are the very mechanisms which further insure that no change will occur. As they feel more hopeless, they engage in "more of the same" tactics which further entrenches them in the harmful consequences of the incest and alcoholism. The more denial they use, the more omnipresent the problem appears, stimulating more prominent denial, and so so. It is much like the proverbial "run-away equation" or "game without end" (Bateson, 1979).

• **Sibling relationships come to be pathologically disturbed.** In the alcoholic and incestuous families, we observe an exceptionally high incidence of disturbed sibling relationships. In each of these families, as one child is elevated to a position of "specialness" and surrogate adult, there is an increase in confusion and frustration. As the "special child" is deprived of the opportunity to experience childhood and engage in age-appropriate activities, the other children feel deprived and "less than special." The ensuing hurt, jealousy, frustration, and inflated or deflated sense of self-esteem which is not age-appropriate, culminates in sibling relationships which are destructive to all involved.

• **An excess of belongingness or separateness to the detriment of the other.** Minuchin (1974) has shown how individuals need to experience a sense of belongingness and a sense of separateness within their family, in order to develop a functional sense of identity and self-esteem. The alcoholic and incestuous family operations provide excesses of one or the other of these important human experiences to the detriment of the other. While some family members have an excessive sense of belongingness, to the point of feeling smothered or suffocated, others experience a sense of separateness amounting to alienation with no source of functional support and nurturance. Neither of these conditions is conducive to the development of healthy, functional individuals. The consequences are shattered, partial people who have pronounced self-doubts and self-esteem problems.

• **Intimacy and trust problems.** As parents in the alcoholic family have their sense of intimacy and trust in one another shattered, their quarrels and difficulties increase. The children observe this decompensation in their parents' conflict resolution skills and relationship. "here the two most significant adult persons in their (children's) life are unable to solve their problems, thereby leaving the children with the generalized belief that this world must indeed be a tenuous place at best," (Barnard, 1981). The children, like their parents, begin to have difficulty feeling comfortable enough to emotionally invest themselves in intimate relationships, generally feel an absence of trust in others, and activate various protective defense mechanisms. The same processes are in operation within the incestuous family. The incest victim feels "special," yet betrayed, while the other children feel "spared," yet unimportant.

• **Dependency issues.** Bowen (1974) has clearly portrayed how alcoholics manifest a lack of ability to function interdependently. Stanton (1982) has similarly documented the excesses of interpersonal dependency observed in alcoholics, and how symbiosis characterizes their relationships. As alcoholics and their family relationships are characterized by dependency problems and an absence of functional and autonomous behavior, the same if true of the incestuous family. Among others, Lustic and his associates (1966) have shown how incestuous families resolve their dependency problems in non-productive ways by identifying the following as a family characteristic: "A fear of family disintegration and abandonment shared by all protagonists, such that any arrangement appears preferable to family disintegration."

Discussion

This article presented characteristics that are observed in both alcoholic and incestuous families. The purpose of these comparisons was to sensitize clinicians who encounter one of these problems to investigate carefully the potential presence of the other. An increase in perceptual powers should presumably result in an increase in accurate diagnosis and treatment. As Bateson has said: "Knowledge at any given moment will be a function of the thresholds of our available means of perception," (1979). Hopefully, this article has increased "thresholds of our available means of perception," such that appropriate and thorough treatment can be brought to bear on these human problems, and much present and future suffering alleviated.

Alcoholism & Incest in the Family—Part II: Issues in Treatment

By Charles P. Barnard, Ed.D.

This article will focus on some significant treatment issues and considerations in relation to families experiencing both alcoholism and incest. Specific ideas will be offered for those who encounter this troubled type of family. Remember, there are many incidents of incest that probably go undetected while families are treated for alcoholism. The counselor treating families where there is alcoholism must be sensitive to the possibility of incest.

The primary focus of this article will be that of father-daughter incest, because of the prominence of this variety in comparison to other configurations. Further, the focus will be that of the family where the father is alcoholic and the mother co-dependent, although incest can, and does, occur in the family where the mother is alcoholic. As suggested in the last article, incest occurs regardless of socio-economic status, race, religious orientation, and other factors that serve to differentiate people into groups.

Reporting and Identification

If not already familiar with one's state statutes regarding the reporting of incest, the reader is well advised to determine the relevant regulations. Generally speaking, a source of this sort of information is the local county social service department. Typically, this is the agency charged to manage these sorts of affairs, and consequently is very sensitive to the state's statutes. Most states now have mandatory reporting laws for professionals who become aware of the occurrence of incest. Recently, there has been an increase in the severity of penalty for not reporting, and certainly it is judicious for the professional counselor to know what is statutorily expected.

It is also wise for professionals to acquaint themselves with local social service and legal representatives who are typically involved in responding to reports of incest. Along with the director of the children's services portion of the county social service operation, the district attorney will typically become involved at the point of reporting. While many areas have well-developed teams and procedures for addressing this very sensitive issue, there are also those who continue to be quite archaic in their response to, and treatment of, incest. By becoming involved with the people who have a statutorily-dictated involvement in responding to incest, it is more reasonable to assume that one will be able to interact with these people in the most productive way possible for the benefit of the client population one serves. There is little doubt of the fact that clients who are served by a counselor who is an active and functional member of the area's human service community receives a better-integrated and overall treatment.

Research has identified a number of characteristics that seem to be correlated with the incidence of incest. While my previous article identified characteristics that are reflective of both alcoholic and incestuous families, the following are specific characteristics that have been found with greater frequency in the family with incest. The reader is advised to be sensitive to these characteristics as clues to the possible presence of incest in the families they treat for alcoholism. They are not offered in order of importance nor significance, and should not be regarded in that fashion.

1. The family with poor mother-daughter connections has been found to be frequently present in incestuous families. The thought is that a strong mother-daughter bond is an excellent source of protection for daughters from possible sexual abuse.

2. Incest and the presence of an alcoholic stepfather have been

found to be highly correlated.

3. Most marriages with a partner who is alcoholic have sexual problems, and this, as well as other frustrations in the adult relationship, can promote incestuous behavior.

4. Incest and physical abuse/corporal punishment are frequently found to occur together. A physically assaultive father should alert the professional to possible incest.

5. A very dependent mother, physically and/or psychologically, is frequently observed in these families. The mother being alcoholic, or suffering from another physical illness, and thus incapacitating her potential protective function, is an important factor for which to be alert. As an example of the level of dependency frequently observed, it is interesting to note the disproportionate incidence of mothers in incestuous families not having earned driver's licenses, with the resultant dependency this fosters.

6. Fathers who have been involved in incest will frequently be observed to be very jealous, and controlling of their daughter's lives. No one is perceived to be "good enough" for his daughters.

7. An "acting out" adolescent girl who seems to have assumed many adult responsibilities in the family context is a possible victim of incest. While incestuous contact usually begins when the child is aged 6-12 years, the behaviors reflective of pronounced parentification, or inappropriate assumption of adult responsibilities, will not manifest themselves until late childhood and/or early adolescence. While the oldest daughter appears to be particularly vulnerable, all other children the father has contact with should be regarded as possible victims. A frequent observation is that as the oldest daughter moves into adolescence, and becomes more capable of resisting and avoiding her father's advances, the younger children become the father's next victims. Similarly, as the adult-child incest becomes more pervasive in the family, there is also a greater incidence of reported sibling incest.

While it is not the writer's intent to suggest that the presence of any one, or all of the above, assure that incest is present in the family, there now is signficant evidence that documents the presence of the above in families where incest exists. Once one observes the above, how does not make a determination? One asks!

While this writer believes it is not appropriate to include questions about child-adult sexual contact in interviews with every family, it is extremely important to explore this factor when the suggestive evidence, in the form of the above indicators, is present. Keep in mind that current data suggest that at least one per cent of all women have had a sexual experience with either a father or stepfather (Finkelhor 1979). While this is true for the general population, there is certainly reason to believe that the rate of incidence is even higher among those families where there is an alcoholic parent. In either case, it appears that the main obstacle to making a determination of incest/sexual abuse, is the interviewer's apprehensiveness. Certainly, this is an area that provokes much affect and resultant reluctance on the part of the professionals.

The denial that is so characteristic of the alcoholic/incestuous family mitigates against this information being spontaneously offered. But just as this is true, it is equally evident that the incest not being identified and treated is a factor weighing against the family ever being able to achieve a really effective recovery process. As an example, untreated incest is likely to result in the adult child who was victimized experiencing chronic self-esteem problems, increased likelihood of repeated victimization, relationship problems and difficulties in developing functional adult sexuality. As the victim experiences these difficulties, other family members including perpetrators, experience more subtle, but nonetheless destructive ramifications.

Once clinicians address the precipitants of their own uneasiness in this area, calm and direct questioning regarding the family's sexual behavior and contacts can occur. In this regard, it is very important to be aware of the low incidence of false reports of incest by children, and consequently the need for being responsive to reports and not discounting them in response to the family's efforts to activate their denial. Given the need for immediate responsiveness and interviewer skill, it is valuable for the clinician to have a personal/professional "cuddle group" available, as well as being sensitized to one's obligations and prerogatives.

Treatment Considerations

Once a report of incest has been received, the clinician must be prepared to be met with massive doses of denial. Decisiveness and pro-activity must characterize the work of the professional. In conjunction with following through with the appropriate reporting strategies, an effort must be expended to protect the reporting child as well as other children in the family. Real variance will be found in this stage, dependent upon the procedures that characterize a particular geographic area. For many years, the standard procedure has been that of immediately removing the reporting child from the home. More recent years have brought on the awareness that this tends to: intensify guilt for the child; lessen the likelihood of beginning to strengthen the mother-daughter bond that is so crucial for future recovery and protection; increase potential for the child to be scapegoated and extricated from the family; promote the likelihood of the father seducing the mother into an alliance with him; and, also create a problem in attempting to find a good placement for the young child. Conversely, if safety cannot be asured at home, the father can utilize options such as a relative or friend's home, or motel, during this initial crisis period. Adults can find shelter much easier than shelter can be located for children, particularly children that are in profound need such as incest victims.

At this time, the entire family is in need of intensive support and assistance. The mother needs support to promote her continuing to be available to the daughter, and other children, just as the reporting daughter needs massive support for her action. While false reports of incest are uncommon, it is not uncommon to observe children who will retract their initial accusation. It is believed that this is not so much because of inaccurate reporting, but rather because of inadequate management by professionals involved. If the child is subject to ridicule, threats of injury, and emotionally becoming ostracized in the absence of support, it is not unreasonable to expect a child to retract a statement. This action can in turn promote even greater calcification of the pathology and dysfunction already present in this family, and lessen hopes for change regarding either the incest or alcoholism. Consequently, the mother and reporting child should receive great support during this initial phase. In all likelihood, the mother will need assistance in believing her daughter at this time, and providing the necessary reassurance to ameliorate the sense of fear and guilt the daughter will likely experience. Without this support, many children may retract their statements, and thus they and their family will become even more unavailable for any type of treatment.

Once the child's statement is reported, and depending upon the geographic/jurisdictional practices, a court order may be issued regarding details of the father's separation from the family while the investigation/treatment is initiated, and also regarding his involvement in treatment. There are various incest treatment programs in the country today that promote a court order in order to insure the father's involvement in both the investigation and treatment process (Giaretto, 1978). This is something clinicians should determine about practices in their own area so that they can act accordingly and in order to insure the best interests of all involved. There is a tremendous need for a coordinated understanding and effort among all professionals involved at this point.

This is frequently a good time to engage the father in inpatient treatment to begin to address the alcoholism as well as the incestuous involvement, and for him to begin to accept the responsibility and consequences. Certainly it would be important to alert the counselors and the inpatient unit to his incestuous behavior so that this also can be addressed. The denial that characterizes both the alcoholic and perpetrator can be effectively addressed in the treatment community. Also, for both the alcoholic and incest perpetrator, the elements of A.A.'s Twelve Steps can be facilitative. Keep in mind that many regard alcoholism and incestuous contact as addictions. One major difference is that the alcoholic eventually develops physical problems, while the perpetrator continues to have his orgasm without the direct effect of physically harmful consequences. In this regard, elements of the Twelve Steps such as addressing the issue of control and powerlessness, conducting a moral self inventory, seeking forgiveness and making amends, are certainly valuable considerations for the perpetrator to be addressing. Just as the Twelve Steps of A.A. have implications for the treatment of incest, so too does the notion of the A.A. sponsor. As the A.A. sponsor can be valuable to the recovering alcoholic when the impulse to drink is present, the sponsor can be similarly valuable to the incest perpetrator when he experiences the inappropriate sexual impulses.

The value of groups for both victims and spouses of perpetrators is rapidly gaining acceptance as a valuable treatment component. In the group context, there is the potential for both support and understanding that the victim and spouse are in such need of. Each can receive support for other 'survivors,' which in and of itself can have such great value. Each can be assisted in understanding the development of incest and the relationship to alcoholism. Also, each can be helped with regard to anger they may harbor in relation to each other, each feeling as though they have been, in various ways, betrayed by the other. The group also provides them the benefit of the principle of universality—they come to realize that they are not alone. They can learn that many others have had these same experiences, and that these are difficulties that can be resolved. Self-help groups such as A.A. have recently developed in response to the problem of incest, and are experiencing great success. The wise clinician will investigate to determine if these groups are available in his/her area. These groups are most frequently referred to as Parents United and Daughters and Sons United.

As it is with alcoholism, so it is with incest (if there is hope for productive resolution and maintenance of the family), that the entire family must receive treatment. All have been affected and the unit must be treated as a whole, not only for rehabilitation, but for prevention as well. Typically the family treatment component will need to be implemented only after stabilization is achieved from the crisis typically provoked by the initial disclosure. Once this stabilization does occur, it is then appropriate, if not essential, to move the treatment to a family focus. The very characteristics of the family that promoted the incest must be addressed in the treatment process. The treatment should focus on the development of more productive and functional connections and behaviors that do not leave room, let alone promote, incestuous and alcoholic behavior (Barnard 1981). Regardless of what one believes are etiological agents to alcoholism and incest, it is evident that the entire family has been affected. Everyone is victimized in varying ways. Changes must now be promoted that stimulate positive self-corrective behaviors to replace those mechanisms that fostered the previous dysfunctions. In this sense, the treatment takes on a preventive, as well as rehabilitative function. Just as we know alcoholism is disproportionately observed among offspring of alcoholics, so too is incest and other forms of abuse found to a disproportionate degree among offspring of abusers. Intervening with the entire family increases the potential for short-circuiting this intergenerational transmission process.

Final Considerations

As mentioned earlier, there is much value in clinicians establishing a "cuddle group" of peers who are available for consultation and support while working with these families. As the denial of the alcoholic family is widely known, we must acknowledge that the taboo against incest is many times greater than the amount of taboo and shame remaining with regard to alcoholism and, consequently, we should expect denial that is at least equal to that observed in the alcoholic family. Struggling with this amount of denial and resultant crises can take its toll and we need to have resources available to help us in this regard. This same "cuddle group" can also help clinicians to identify their own countertransference issues in the form of reactions and attitudes held toward perpetrators, incest and the issue of abuse in general. Without remaining sensitive to our own issues, the risk exists for us to provide treatment that is more responsive to our personal issues than to the multitude of needs presented by these families. It seems essential for us to acknowledge that incest is a human problem that probably possesses greater capacity for provoking our own personal biases than any other problem we might encounter, and subsequently take preventive measures for all concerned.

Relapse—The Family's Involvement
PartI: Post Acute Withdrawal

By Terence T. Gorski and Merlene Miller

"Now that she finally stopped drinking, everything will be all right." This is what many family members believe when the alcoholic enters treatment. After all, wasn't drinking the cause of all the problems? And now that she is not drinking, won't she become the person we have always wanted her to be? Unfortunately, the answer is an emphatic "no." There are three reasons why the alcoholic and the family don't simply return to normal.

First, alcoholism is a chronic disease, and those suffering from it are prone to relapse. It does not just go away when the drinking stops. The alcoholic experiences symptoms that persist into recovery. The most common of these are symptoms of a neurological condition called post acute withdrawal (PAW).

Second, the spouse and family members of the alcoholic develop a condition called co-alcoholism as a direct result of living in a committed relationship with the alcoholic. Co-alcoholism does not just go away when the alcoholic stops drinking. Family members must recognize that they have become co-alcoholic and initiate a recovery program before they can recover. Co-alcoholism causes the family members to react in a confusing and chaotic manner to the alcoholic. These reactions may contribute to the relapse potential.

Third, there is a powerful "no-talk rule" surrounding the issue of relapse. Many, if not most, alcoholics return to alcohol or drug use at least once after they attempt permanent sobriety. The alcoholic has tried to stay sober and failed many times. The family has lived through many such attempts. Their hopes have soared only to be destroyed by the alcoholic's return to alcohol or drug use. They lack confidence in the alcoholic's ability to recover, but are afraid to talk about their fears because they believe their lack of faith may contribute to a relapse. They pretend there is no problem and do not face the possibility of relapse.

This is the first of three articles that will explore what happens to the alcoholic and family members that creates the risk of relapse. The articles will also present recommendations to the alcoholic and family members for learning how to avoid relapse.

Alcoholics do not suddenly return to normal when they stop drinking. The drinking-based symptoms of alcoholism go away, but they are replaced by the sobriety-based symptoms. Alcoholism is a disease. The body of the alcoholic responds to alcohol differently from the body of the non-alcoholic. As a result, alcohol has a toxic effect upon the brain and nervous system. Damage to the brain and nervous system does not correct itself rapidly. Full recovery from the neurological consequences of alcoholism requires a period of 6 to 24 months. Worst of all, full recovery does not mean that the alcoholic is normal. It simply means that he or she has learned to manage the sobriety-based symptoms well enough to be able to live a normal life with the assistance of a structured recovery program.

During periods of high stress, a cluster of symptoms called post acute withdrawal will become reactivated. The family's response to these post acute withdrawal symptoms will be critical in raising or lowering the risk of relapse. If the family is locked into untreated co-alcoholism, they will tend to react unappropriately to these symptoms. Their reactions may be harsh, punitive, or irrational. As a result, they can aggravate the symptoms and drive the alcoholic one step closer to drinking.

Post acute withdrawal (PAW) is a syndrome or a collection of symptoms that develops after the alcoholic has stopped alcohol/ drug use and recovered from the symptoms of acute withdrawal. These symptoms include the inability to think clearly, the inability to generate clear and appropriate emotional reactions, and the inability to remember recent events. The symptoms are stress sensitive and become worse when the alcoholic is not well-rested, not eating well-balanced meals, and is fatigued or under pressure.

The symptoms of PAW are not psychological. They result from chronic brain and nervous system damage caused by alcoholism. The symptoms are very similar to the symptoms exhibited by a person who has suffered a mild stroke or a head injury. Let's review these symptoms in more detail and then discuss the family's role in helping the patient to cope with these symptoms.

The first category of symptoms is thought process disorders: the inability to think clearly. The alcoholic will show the symptoms of thought process impairment in several different ways. At times, alcoholics experience periods when their minds begin to race. They have rigid and repetitive thoughts that they can't stop. Their minds keep reviewing the same thoughts over and over in seemingly endless cycles. The alcoholic recognizes that this is inappropriate and does not like what is happening, but simply cannot stop it.

At other times, alcoholics will be unable to construct logical chains of thought. They cannot figure things out step by step, even very simple things. They feel that they cannot get their brains started. At other times they appear to be thinking clearly but judgment is impaired. They think they have the answer, but it turns out to be wrong. They believe they know how to solve a problem, but when they attempt to solve it, they just make things worse. Their judgment is bad because the brain centers that control abstract thinking, cause/effect determination, and concentration simply are not working properly. They cannot recognize patterns or determine cause and effect relationships. They cannot understand concepts that are complex or abstract.

The second type of symptom is emotional process impairment. The alcoholic's ability to generate clear and appropriate emotional responses to situations is damaged. At times they will over-react. This is called augmentation. It is caused by malfunction of the nervous system. The brain and nerves discharge too much energy in response to a stimulus. If the brain can be compared to an adding machine, it is like having one key stuck down all the time.

At other times, alcoholics become emotionally numb. Feelings and emotions shut off. As a result, they do not have emotional reactions, even when they think they should. They may love their family but not feel the love emotionally. They may be in trouble at work, but not feel upset. Someone yells at them, but they feel no anger. Why don't they react? They can't, because the brain is not allowing emotional reactions to occur.

Recovering persons can also experience emotions unexpectedly for no apparent reason. The brain can suddenly fire off and produce an emotional reaction that has nothing to do with what is going on. The alcoholic can be at work and suddenly become frightened. Or talking to a friend casually and suddenly become angry. Or feel anxious and nervous for no reason. If alcoholics do not recognize that these inappropriate or "crazy" feelings are caused by the sobriety-based neurological symptoms of alcoholism, they can come to believe that they are crazy, or attempt to find justifications for their feelings by blaming people or situations around them for "making me feel this way."

Recovering alcoholics also have difficulty with short-term memory. Many memories tend to dissolve within 15 to 20 minutes. The harder they try to remember, the faster they forget. This is not intentional. The brain process that transfers short-term memory into long-term memory has been damaged by the alcoholism. As a result, the memories simply do not get stored.

The most confusing and aggravating part of PAW is that it is intensified by stress. When alcoholics are well rested, eating properly, and maintaining healthy communication with other people, they appear to be fine. Their thoughts are clear, their emotions appropriate, and their memory all right. At times of high stress, however, the brain suddenly shuts down. They become confused. The mind starts racing. They overreact and then just numb out. At times they feel strange or crazy feelings for no reason at all. When they calm down and try to relax and sort it all out, they find they cannot remember exactly what happened.

Many alcoholics think that they are going crazy and they deny or attempt to hide these reactions from family and friends. If family members, friends, employers, and co-workers do not recognize that these symptoms are neurological in origin and not a deliberate conscious behavior, they can overreact to or misinterpret the symptoms. What can family members do to learn how to cope with the alcoholic and symptoms of PAW?

1. **Understand that alcoholism is a neurological disease that doesn't go away with abstinence.** It is important that family members understand that the alcoholic has a neurological disease that doesn't go away with abstinence, that this disease produces specific symptoms of a post acute withdrawal syndrome. PAW symptoms are not intentional and at times are so severe that the alcoholic cannot control them.

2. **Recognize that confrontation and conflict will only make the symptoms worse.** To confront or punish the alcoholic for showing symptoms of PAW will only make things worse. PAW is aggravated by stress. The higher the stress, the worse the symptoms. It is more beneficial to support, understand, and help set up a treatment plan with the help of a professional counselor who understands PAW and its treatment.

3. **Recognize and treat co-alcoholism in all family members.** Anyone who has been living in a long-term committed relationship with an alcoholic will develop co-alcoholism. Co-alcoholism is marked by the need to control the alcoholic and other people and situations. It is also marked by chaotic emotional and behavioral reactions. It does not go away when the alcoholic stops drinking. Co-alcoholic responses can make PAW worse and contribute to the risk of relapse.

4. **Give the alcoholic room to recover.** Family members should develop interests and friends that are not dependent upon the alcoholic. The need to give themselves permission to get away.

5. **Acknowledge and discuss the PAW symptoms.** Break the "No-Talk Rule" by acknowledging and openly discussing the symptoms of PAW and developing methods for coping with those symptoms.

6. **Involve the alcoholic in understanding co-alcoholism and its symptoms.** Let the alcoholic know that the family has problems and difficulties. Expect the alcoholic to make an effort to understand and support recovery from co-alcoholism. This allows all family members to learn and grow.

7. Be patient. Accept that recovery will take time and don't become frustrated by setting unrealistic expectations.

8. Set up a formal relapse prevention plan for both alcoholism and co-alcoholism. The family needs to work with a counselor to establish a formal relapsc prevention plan that will allow family members to support recovery in each other and help to intervene should the relapse warning symptoms get out of control.

Relapse-The Family's Involvement PartII: Co-Alcoholism Factors

By Terence T. Gorski and Merlene Miller

The family's involvement in the relapse syndrome is strongly influenced by co-alcoholism.

Co-alcoholism is a primary condition that results from the debilitating physiological stress produced by living in a committed relationship with an alcoholic or drug dependent person. The physiological stress is produced by the regular interaction of the family with the symptoms of alcoholism or drug dependence. It is important to remember that there are both alcohol and drug-induced symptoms, and withdrawal-induced symptoms. The alcoholic doesn't return to normal when s/he stops drinking. The long term withdrawal, called Post Acute Withdrawal (PAW), can persist for six months to two years into sobriety. As a result, co-alcoholism can be aggravated by the symptoms of PAW.

The person suffering from co-alcoholism develops physical, psychological, behavioral, and social symptoms as a result of attempting to adapt to and compensate for the debilitating effects of the physiological stress. As co-alcoholism progresses, the stress-related symptoms become habitual. The symptoms occur automatically and unconsciously. The symptoms also become self-reinforcing, that is, the presence of one co-alcoholic symptom will automatically trigger others. The co-alcoholism eventually becomes independent of the alcoholism or drug dependence that originally caused it. The symptoms of co-alcoholism will continue, even if the alcoholic becomes sober, or if the co-alcoholic ends the relationship with the alcoholic.

The term "co-alcoholism" is sometimes used to refer only to the spouse of an alcoholic, and other terms such as "para-alcoholic" are being used to refer to children. In this article, the term "co-alcoholic" is used to refer to **ANYONE WHOSE LIFE HAS BECOME UNMANAGEABLE AS A RESULT OF LIVING IN A COMMITTED RELATIONSHIP WITH AN ALCOHOLIC.**

Co-alcoholism is a definite and definable syndrome that is chronic and follows a predictable progression. When persons living in a committed relationship with an alcoholic attempt to control drinking and drinking behavior (over which they are powerless), they lose control over their own behavior (over which they **can** have the power) and their lives become unmanageable.

EARLY STAGE: Normal Problem Solving and Attempts to Adjust to Heavy Drinking.

Co-alcoholism results from the excessively high stress caused by living in a committed relationship with an alcoholic. Developing slowly at first, the co-alcoholic comes to accept the alcoholic's heavy drinking as normal. As problems develop, they attempt to use normal, culturally-defined problem-solving and coping mechanisms to deal with the symptoms of alcoholism. The symptoms of alcoholism do not respond to these methods. As a matter of fact, most normal, family problem-solving and coping mechanisms will support, or actually increase (enable) the level of alcoholism symptoms.

The normal reaction within any family to pain, crisis, and to the dysfunction of one member of the family is to reduce the pain, ease the crisis, and to assist the dysfunctional member in order to protect the family. These reponses do not make things better when the problem is alcoholism, because these measures deprive the alcoholic of the painful learning experiences that bring an awareness that alcohol is creating problems in his or her life. At this stage, the co-alcoholism is simply a reaction to the symptoms of the disease of alcoholism. It is a normal response to an abnormal situation.

MIDDLE STAGE: The Development of Habitual Self-Defeating Coping Mechanisms.

When the culturally-prescribed responses to stress and crises do not bring relef from the pain created by the alcoholism in the family, the concerned persons **TRY HARDER**. They do more of the same things; more often, more intensely, more desperately. They try to be more supportive, more helpful, more protective. They take on responsibilities of the alcoholic, not realizing that this causes the alcoholic to become irresponsible.

The responses to drinking and drinking behavior become habitual, fixated, and unconscious mechanisms for coping with the problem. They do the same things they have always done, even though those responses are not working. They adapt their own behavior and the functioning of the family to accommodate the drinking. But, things get worse instead of better, and the sense of failure intensifies the response. They experience frustration, anxiety and guilt. There is growing self-blame, self-concept degeneration, and self-defeating behaviors. The co-alcoholic becomes isolated. Their focus is on drinking and drinking behavior and inefficacious attempts to control these. They have little time to focus on anything else. The result is further removal from the world outside of their alcoholic family.

CHRONIC STAGE: Family Collapse and Stress Degenerations

The continued, habitual response to alcoholism in the family results in specific, repetitive, circular patterns of self-defeating behavior. These behavior patterns are independent and self-reinforcing, persisting even in the absence of continued alcoholism symptomatology.

The things the family members have done in a sincere effort to help have failed, and the resulting despair and guilt bring about confusion, chaos, and the inability to interrupt dysfunctional behavior ... even when they are aware that it is not helping. The thinking and behavior of the co-alcoholic is **out-of-control**, and these patterns will continued, even if the alcoholic gets sober, dies, or is separated from the family.

Co-alcoholic degeneration is physical, psychological, behavioral, social, and spiritual. The ineffective attempts to control drinking and drinking behavior elevate chronic stress to the point of producing stress-related **physical** illnesses such as migraine headaches, ulcers, and hypertension. This chronic stress may also result in nervous breakdown or other emotional or psychological illnesses. Out-of-control behavior manifests itself in an alcoholism-centered lifestyle that pervades all life activity, even that which seems unrelated to drinking or drinking behavior. Social degeneration occurs as the alcoholism focus interferes with relationships and social activity within and outside of the family. Spiritual degeneration results as the focus on the problem becomes so pervasive that there is no interest in anything beyond it, particularly concerns and needs related to a higher meaning of life.

Recovery from Co-Alcoholism

Recovery from co-alcoholism means learning to accept and detach from the symptoms of alcoholism and learning to manage and control the symptoms of co-alcoholism. It means learning to focus on personal needs and personal growth, learning to respect and like oneself. It means learning to choose appropriate behavior. It means learning to be in control of one's life.

Because it is a chronic condition, co-alcoholism, like alcoholism, is subject to relapse. But conditions of co-alcoholic relapse may be more difficult to identify. Without an ongoing recovery program and proper care of oneself, old feelings and behaviors thought to be under control may surface and become out of control. Life again becomes unmanageable; **the co-alcoholic is in relapse**. The symptoms of the "Co-alcoholic Crisis" and the warning signs that precede it, are listed on the accompanying chart entitled *Relapse Warning Signs for Co-Alcoholism.*

Co-Alcoholism and Relapse

While each family member is responsible for his own recovery, the symptoms of alcoholism and co-alcoholism each impact upon the relapse potential of the other. Even if the alcoholic is no longer drinking and no longer experiencing the drinking-related symptoms of the disease, the post-acute withdrawal symptoms (PAW) affect and are affected by co-alcoholism. Both the symptoms of post acute withdrawal and the symptoms of co-alcoholism are stress sensitive. Stress intensifies the symptoms and the symptoms intensify stress. As a result, the alcoholic and the co-alcoholic can become a stress-generating team that unknowingly and unconsciously complicate each other's recovery and create a high risk of relapse.

When a recovering co-alcoholic does not understand or recognize the symptoms of post acute withdrawal being experienced by the recovering alcoholic, these symptoms can trigger a stress reaction that can lead to relapse for the entire family. The pattern is as follows:

1. The PAW symptoms of the alcoholic cause stress in the co-alcoholic.
2. The intensified stress in the co-alcoholic produces the early warning signs of a co-alcoholic crisis.
3. The co-alcoholic crisis triggers the early warning signs of relapse in the alcoholic.
4. The relapse warning signs produce even more stress for the co-alcoholic, and a full-blown co-alcoholic crisis ensues, marked by agitated, unpredictable and disruptive mood swings and behaviors.
4. The relapse warning signs produce even more stress for the co-alcoholic, and a full-blown co-alcoholic crisis ensues, marked by agitated, unpredictable and disruptive mood swings and behaviors.
5. The stress of living with a family member in active co-alcoholic crisis increases the stress levels of the alcoholic and causes the alcoholic relapse syndrome to get worse.
6. Both the alcoholic and the co-alcoholic eventually become incapacitated.

What can family members do to reduce the risk of their own relapse and the risk of relapse in the alcoholic?

1. Become informed about the disease of alcoholism, recovery, and the symptoms that accompany recovery.
2. Recognize the symptoms of post acute withdrawal as sobriety-based symptoms of alcoholism when they occur, rather than character defects, emotional disturbances, or mental illness.
3. Accept and recognize the symptoms of co-alcoholism, your reaction to alcoholism in the family.
4. Become involved in Al-Anon and/or your own therapy, and develop a plan for your own recovery.
5. Learn to protect yourself from the stress that may be generated by the symptoms of post acute withdrawal experienced by the recovering alcoholic.

6. Cooperate in plans to protect the recovering alcoholic from stress created by symptoms of co-alcoholism.

7. Be patient with your own recovery and the recovery of the alcoholic. None of you became ill overnight, and recovery will take place over a long period of time.

8. Recognize the relapse potential of alcoholism and co-alcoholism.

9. Develop a plan to prevent your own relapse and support relapse prevention plans for the alcoholic.

Relapse Warning Signs for Co-Alcoholism

Early Warning Signs

Situational loss of daily structure.
Lack of personal care.
Inability to set and stick with limits with children.
Loss of constructive planning.
Indecision.
Compulsive behaviors.
Fatigue or lack of rest.
Return of unreasonable resentments.
Return of tendency to control people, situations, and things.
Defensiveness.
Self-pitying.
Overspending.
Eating disorders—over or under.
Scapegoating.

Acute Co-Alcoholic Crisis

Return of fear and general anxiety.
Loss of belief in a "Higher Power."
Attendance at formal support meetings becomes sporadic.
Mind racing.
Inability to construct a logical chain of thought.
Confusion.
Sleep disturbances.
Artifact emotion.
Behavioral loss of control.
Uncontrollable mood swings.
Failure to maintain interpersonal (informal) support systems.
Feelings of loneliness, isolation.
Tunnel vision.
Return of periods of free-floating anxiety and/or panic attacks.
Health problems.
Use of medication or alcohol as a means to cope.
Total abandonment of support meetings, therapy sessions.

Debilitation

Inability to change behaviors in spite of conscious awareness that it is self-defeating.
Development of an "I don't care" attitude.
Complete loss of daily structure.
Despair and suicidal ideation.
Major physical collapse.
Major emotional collapse.

Relapse—The Family's Involvement Part III: Protocol for Long-Term Recovery

By Terence T. Gorski and Merlene Miller

Relapse Prevention Planning (RPP), is a method for interrupting the progressive symptoms of relapse in both the alcoholic and co-alcoholic. The RPP Protocol was originally developed by Alcoholism Systems Associates, the CENAPS Corporation, in 1975. It was initially designed to prevent relapse in the alcoholic only.

Clinical experience with RPP in a variety of treatment programs indicated that the family could be a powerful ally in preventing relapse in the alcoholic. In 1980, the RPP Protocol was modified to include the involvement of significant others, including family members. This strengthened the effectiveness of RPP significantly. With further clinical experience, however, other problems became apparent. Many family members refused to participate in relapse prevention planning. Other family members participated in a manner that was counter-productive. The spouse was often over-controlling, punitive, or simply failed to follow through in the agreed manner.

These problems were caused, in large part, because the family members were suffering from undiagnosed and untreated co-alcoholism.

In 1983, the RPP protocol was expanded to include relapse prevention in both the alcoholic and the co-alcoholic. In many cases, the alcoholic is the first family member to seek treatment. Other family members become involved in treatment in order to get the alcoholic sober. Many family members refuse to consider the fact that they have a problem with co-alcoholisma that requires specialized treatment. These family members tend to deny their role in the alcoholic family and scapegoat personal and family problems upon the alcoholic. They develop unrealistic expectations that family life will improve with the alcoholic's recovery. When these expectations are not met, they will tend to blame the alcoholic for the failure, even though he may be successfully following a recovery program. Their attitude and behaviors can complicate the alcoholic's recovery and can contribute to relapse.

The newly-designed RPP Protocol utilizes the family's motivation to get the alcoholic sober. As family members become involved in relapse prevention planning, a strong focus is placed upon co-alcoholism and its role in family relapse. Family members are helped to recognize their own co-alcoholism and become actively involved in their own treatment. Alcoholism is presented as a family disease that affects all family members. All family members require treatment. The alcoholic needs treatment for alcoholism. Other family members need treatment for co-alcoholism.

Acute Relapse Episodes

All members of an alcoholic family are prone to return to self-defeating behaviors that can cause them to become dysfunctional. This is described as an **acute relapse episode.** An acute relapse episode can occur with an alcoholic or a co-alcoholic family member.

Not all acute relapse episodes in the alcoholic involve alcohol and drug use. Many alcoholics, for example, develop serious problems as a result of the post acute withdrawal (PAW) syndrome, even though they never use alcohol or drugs. In the same manner, the co-alcoholic often becomes dysfunctional even though the alcoholic is sober and working an active recovery program. This period of dysfunction in the co-alcoholic is known as a co-alcoholic crisis.

Family Relapse Prevention Planning (RPP) has the following goals:

1. To prevent acute relapse episodes in the alcoholic;
2. To prevent co-alcoholic crisis in the co-alcoholic;
3. To develop a relapse prevention plan for both the alcoholic and the co-alcoholic, should they show warning signs of becoming dysfunctional or developing serious problems;
4. To develop an early intervention plan to interrupt acute relapse episodes in both the alcoholic and the co-alcoholic. For the alcoholic, this involves interrupting problems that are caused both by the post acute withdrawal (PAW) syndrome (in the sober alcoholic), or by alcohol or drug use (in the alcoholic) who has returned to drinking and/or drug use. For the co-alcoholic, this involves interrupting the co-alcoholic crisis.

The Family RPP Protocol consists of 12 basic procedures:

- **Stabilization:** The first step in relapse prevention planning is to stabilize both the alcoholic and the co-alcoholic. The alcoholic is stabilized through the process of detoxification or treatment of PAW. The spouse is stabilized by a process of treating the co-alcoholic crisis through: detachment from the alcoholic crisis; regaining a reality-based perspective; and the development of some basic strengths. This often requires attendence at both Al-Anon and professional counseling.
- **Assessment:** Prior to developing a relapse prevention plan, it is necessary to evaluate the alcoholic, the co-alcoholics, and the family system. The evaluation should assess the current problems of family members, their willingness and ability to initiate their own personal recovery programs, and their willingness to become involved in a program of family recovery.
- **Education:** Accurate information is the most powerful of all recovery tools. The alcoholic and the family must learn about alcoholism, the condition of co-alcoholism, treatment, and relapse prevention planning. This education is best provided to the family unit in multiple-family classes. It is helpful if the education is accompanied by separate group therapy programs for each family member. The alcoholic should enter an alcoholic group, the adult co-alcoholic should enter a spouse's group, and the children should enter a children's group. It is in these group treatment sessions that individual recovery of all family members is initiated.

• **Warning Sign Identification:** Both the alcoholic and the co-alcoholic need to identify the personal warning signs that indicate that they are becoming dysfunctional. A personal list of warning signs needs to be written clearly and concisely by the recovering persons. The warning signs must be concrete, specific, and observable by other persons. A good relapse warning sign answers two questions: How will I know when I'm in trouble with recovery? And, how will other people know when I'm in trouble with my recovery?

• **Family Validation of Warning Signs:** After each family member has developed a personal list of warning signs and reviewed these in his group, a series of family sessions is scheduled. During these sessions, each family member presents his personal list of warning signs and asks for feedback. Other family members discuss the warning signs and help assess if they are specific and observable. New warning signs may be added to the list, based upon the feedback of other family members. Since each family member has a list of warning signs that precedes acute relapse episodes, there is no identified patient. All family members participate from a position of equality. They are saying to each other, "We have all been equally affected by alcoholism."

• **Review of the Recovery Program.** Each family member will report to the rest of the family the recovery program thta he has established. The focus here is: How will you and I know that I am doing well in my recovery? Each is invited to express his recovery needs and point ot his progress in treatment.

• **Inventory Training:** All members of the family receive training in how to complete a morning planning inventory and an evening review inventory. These focus heavily upon time structuring, realistic goal setting, and problem solving.

• **Communication Training:** The family members must learn to communicate effectively in order for RPP to work. The family is trained in the process of giving and receiving feedback in a constructive and caring manner.

• **The Family Relapse Prevention Plan:** Family members discuss each of their warning signs, how the family has dealt with those warning signs in the past, and what strategies could be effectively used in the future. Future situations in which the warning signs are likely to be encountered are identified. Strategies for more effective management of the warning signs for each process,. a great deal of role playing and problem-solving occur. Problems are often identified that are taken back to the separate therapy groups for further work.

• **Denial Interruption Plan:** Both alcoholism and co-alcoholism are diseases of denial. Most of the denial is unconsicous. The person doesn't realize he is in denial when it is happening. It is important to take the reality of denial into account early in the RPP process. Each family member should be asked the question: What are other people in your family supposed to do if they give you feedback about concrete warning signs and you deny them, ignore the feedback, or become angry and upset? Each family member should recommend specific strategies for dealing with his own denial. The open discussion sets the stage for intervention, should denial become a problem in the future.

• **The Relapse Early Intervention Plan:** Alcoholism and co-alcoholism are prone to relapse. Relapse means becoming dysfunctional in recovery. For the alcoholic, relapse may involve alcohol and drug use, or it may simply mean that the person becomes so depressed, anxious, angry, or upset that he is dysfunctional in sobriety. For the co-alcoholic, relapse means the return of an out-of-control-state that interferes with normal functioning. Once family members enter an acute relapse episode they are out of control of their thoughts, emotions, judgments, and behavior. They often need the direct help of other family members to interrupt the crisis. Many times they resist this help and act as if they don't want help, even when they desperately need it.

The family is instructed in the process of intervention. Intervention is a method of helping people who don't want to be helped. This intervention training has resulted in a radical decrease in the duration and severity of relapse episodes in family members.

• **Follow-up and Reinforcement.** Alcoholism and co-alcoholism are life-long conditions. They can go into remission, but they never totally disappear. They rest quietly waiting for a lapse in the recovery program to become active again. It is important that the family maintain an ongoing recovery program including A.A., Al-Anon, and periodic relapse prevention check-ups with a professional alcoholism counselor.

H. Stephen Glenn Speaks on Family's Reassertion of Influence on Children

The following article is reprinted from *The U.S. Journal of Drug and Alcohol Dependence.*

By H. Stephen Glenn

After more than three decades of steady deterioration, the American family is starting again to assert itself as a productive force in the development of its children, an authority on family life told the Fourth Annual Conference on Alcoholism and Chemical Dependency, sponsored by the Annenberg Center for Health Sciences and the Betty Ford Center of the Eisenhower Medical Center.

H. Stephen Glenn, Ph.D., Vice President, Humansphere, and President of the Family Development Institute, Washington, D.C., said the development of family life courses, school and church-based parent and family counseling services, pastoral counseling for families, and the creation of support networks for families, has sharply reversed the trend to deterioration which began when millions of women left farms and small towns to work in wartime factories—never to return to the families in which they were nurtured.

Glenn noted that one of the most significant signs of family life regeneration has been the development of more than 4,700 self-help parent groups to deal with just the issue drug abuse.

These are the kinds of activities, said Glenn, that may help modern society replace the support and supervision systems lost in the breakdown of the family circle. The young people of the post war years made up the first generation of parents to ever attempt to establish families and to train children for adulthood with no active involvement "of grandmas, grandpas, aunts, uncles, nieces, neighbors, in-laws and friends." It was also the first "to raise and educate an entire generation of children without even parents involved in the process most of the time," he added.

Immediately after World War II, said Glenn, more than five million young women who had left farms and small towns to work in war production factories decided to stay on in the cities and "ensure for their children ... all the things they did without."

"Out of love they committed to the greatest binge of materialism any generation had ever committed to. And they did it because they saw material things as love, not knowing that their children, who wouldn't know the contrast, might not interpret it that way.'

History shows that five million marriages were performed in 1946—many of them involving former rural dwellers with no previous experience in the outside world, said Glenn.

"They were getting married in the highest hopes that by sparing their children anything that approached hard work, sacrifice, insecurity, or ... reality in any form ... they (the children) would become the greatest flock of eagles ever seen on earth."

Instead, said Glenn, "they became constipated chickens ... spending more time clucking around than flying boldly into the future."

Through 1946 and '47, 11 million families were formed, embracing some 77 million people, said Glenn. It was a "fertility binge" that would last almost 20 years. And in most cases, the families moved away from their "family" homes, sometimes going great distances, ending up in isolation from their friends, former family supports, the "networks" that had been so intimately involved in the rearing of children throughout history.

Without these family supports, and without recourse to the

wisdom borne of experience, what did these young families do?

"They read books, they placed their trust in the published words of 'theorists who had never raised children themselves, but had appropriate degrees,' (so that everybody figured they must have known what they were talking about."

What did these books tell them?

Some said, "Don't spank the kids, you could ruin their creativity."

Others said, "Never contaminate their (children's) thinking with a point of view ... let them float to 21 and do their thing, whatever that involves."

Still others said, "Never risk doing lasting psychological damage by saying 'no.' "

People have always accumulated wisdom about raising families from families themselves. But in the great uprooting of young people after the Second World War, the chance to develop that wisdom didn't occur. And so young parents were left virtually on their own. Books and theorists became the substitute for "grandmas, grandpas, aunts, uncles, and friends," said Glenn.

This was so not only for the accumulation of knowledge about families, but for the responsibility for supervision.

"If a local shopkeeper stepped in and corrected my son, I went and thanked him for it. I didn't sue him, the way we tend to do today," said Glenn.

But that system of supporting and looking out for each other and each other's children was "suddenly wiped out." What was left was a vacuum, to be filled with a lot of conflicting and often misguided theories which negated many of the child-rearing principles "that had helped us for thousands of years," said Glenn.

Perhaps the key in the relearning process is the realization that even young children need to feel a role and sense of resposibility within the family circle, said Glenn. They are not just passive receivers of gifts. They have to feel there is a purpose to their lives, they have to feel they are important to others, and that things are expected of them as members of a family.

"Research shows," said Glenn, "that the rise in violent crimes, teenage pregnancy, drug and alcohol abuse, and teenage suicide is (directly related to) a lack of perception of meaning, purpose, significance, relevant status ... the frustration of living endlessly in an insignificant way in a place that you're not needed, not taken seriously, not important to the process ..."

Yet many parents encourage that perception of insignificance by showering their children with gifts intead of their time, by allowing them freedom to "do their own thing," rather than establishing clear guidelines and rules that are applied fairly and consistently.

"We've begun to discover (again) that young people still do need that (parental) contact and even want it most of the time," said Glenn.

But in the absence of grandparents, relatives, caring neighbors, those contacts become diluted. And so parents must make extra efforts to establish and maintain them.

Glenn noted that 82% of all American children "will come home tonight to a family where every living member has given their best shot 10 hours a day somewhere else."

That child, added Glenn, will come back to a household "where none of the routine business is out of the way," where the parent or parents must run fast to get food on the table, "to sort out clothes, to get a couple of chores taken care of, can have a warning or two issued, and maybe have a few moments in the tub.

"Where in that process," said Glenn, "(is the time) to pass on wisdom, judgment, insight, morals, ethics, principles, self discipline, responsibility, a sense of meaning, purpose, significance, relevance, and status ... all the things that children must possess?"

Glenn added that the post war generation of parents was the first to try to raise a generation of children "whose on the job training for life doesn't include life, but is more likely to include a family room dominated by a machine that portrays drinking, self medication, casual sexuality, and expedient violence as the essential tools for happy, productive adulthood."

The result of this abandonment of family in the post war years, said Glenn, allowed "epidemics of teenage suicide, drug abuse, violent crime, teenage pregnancy, and underachievement."

He added that in 1982, four out of every 20 girls in the 13 to 20 age group in the United States was pregnant for some part of the year. And although the majority of them either had an abortion or aborted spontaneously, enough followed through to produce one million children out of wedlock to teenage mothers in 1982.

The greatest increase in motherhood also occurred among girls aged 15 to 15½, compared to all other teenage groups.

In all of these areas, "we have set world records," said Glenn. He noted that the only "challenger" for any of these records would be Japan, where teenage suicide is also rampant, although suicide in Japan is viewed more as an act of honor (for failure to excel or match expectations), than it is an act of shame or desperation.

The legacy of this quest for material goods at the expense of family structure has been ruinous, said Glenn.

"Basically, affluence has done to the teenager in America what paternalism did to the native American or Indian 20 years earlier with the same basic symptoms: lack of motivation and achievement, increasing depression, disillusionment, suidice, chemical dependency.

"Fortunately," said Glenn, "the resurgence of interest in family dynamics through the formation of family life groups has allowed quantum leaps forward in understanding ourselves."

From 'Reconstruction' to 'Restoration' Experiential Intervention for Families and Adult Children of Alcoholics

By Sharon Wegscheider

Not long ago, I ran across a definition of experience as "history plus feelings." Perhaps the experience most common to every culture is that its children grow up in **families**—be they nuclear, extended, or communal. Obviously, the family has a profound effect on the kinds of adults we become. What, then, happens when children grow up in dysfunctional families such as those touched by alcoholism?

For myself, I know the answer. My family "history" is full of episodes associated with my parents' alcoholism. The "feelings" I had were a confused mixture of guilt, shame and hurt when they were drinking, and love, comfort and security when they were sober. At either emotional pole, I had to wonder if I weren't crazy to feel so pulled apart in my emotional life.

I responded to all this by being super-responsible so that I could be a rallying point for my parents, younger brother and sister. I worked to be popular, became the star of the Debate Team and the apple of my father's eye. I succeeded in becoming the Family Princess, and yet my parents' drinking persisted. The message: **Try harder!**

Small wonder, then, that the driving force of my adult life was to "try harder." And still, I could never be satisfied with anything I did. Life for me seemed an endless series of efforts that fell short; I was striving for an ideal that did not exist!

My own cycle of despair and confusion was broken several years ago by my "Reconstruction" with Virginia Satir. On that day, she guided me through a tableau of events from my family's past, lovingly re-enacted by her other students. With their support, I relived my childhood and felt, once again, the fear and confusion of seeing my parents fight at the dinner table, of seeing my father "asleep" on the floor, of feeling my mother's love and support for me drained under the pressures of the illness of alcoholism. I relived my teenage and young adult years through recreation of other vignettes culled from my memory.

When the "Reconstruction" ended, I had relived a lifetime of pain. I had re-felt my feelings, discarded the ones which were no longer appropriate or useful, and paused a moment to cherish the ones which were no longer appropriate or useful, and paused a moment to cherish the ones that had given me pleasure. I made many choices the day of my "Reconstruction." And while I would stop short of saying that I was reborn a healthy choicemaker in the space of that one day, I will say—unequivocally—that that experience turned my life around so that I could rebuild from a healthy base. I took control of my life, rather than to continue being controlled by feelings triggered by the illness of "co-dependency."

Today, one of the greatest joys of my life is guiding other people through "Family Reconstruction" so that they too may leave old issues behind and become healthy choicemakers.

Virginia Satir's "Reconstruction" of me was of her very special style, and I am indebted to her. In the intervening years, I have evolved my own style of "Reconstruction" based upon additional knowledge we have learned from alcoholic families. This process has changed in many ways; and in order to separate and clarify the two processes, my "Reconstructions" in the future will be referred to as **"Family Restoration."**

* * * * * * * * * * * * * * * * * *

The workshop always begins on a Sunday evening. At this

point, most of the participants are strangers to each other. Each person introduces himself to the group and may talk about his personal goals over the next four days. The evening of introduction is always special to me, because I know that this group of strangers will know each other like family before the week is over.

Monday is a day of learning about alcoholism, drug abuse, family systems and birth order. My professional life has been dedicated to changing or cultural and political views of alcoholism. It is not merely the disease of the Dependent person (the afflicted); it is a family disease and a primary disease within every member of the affected family. When chemical addiction occurs in one family member, the other members adapt to that person's unstable behavior by developing behavior of their own that causes the least amount of personal stress. This protects each person's feeling life, so the family survives—but only the most sick and deluded survival.

I talk about the family roles that I saw emerge in my own clinical experience: **The Enabler**—(usually the spouse who does "everything under the sun" to make the drinking spouse stop except what works: confronting the user or leaving the relationship. Enabling behavior is habitual; it will endure after separation from the Dependent unless treated); **The Family Hero** (who sees and hears what is happening and takes responsibility for the family pain by becoming successful and popular); **The Family Scapegoat** (who rejects the family system by running away, withdrawal, or defiant behavior); **The Lost Child** (who quietly and unobtrusively withdraws from the family system); and **The Mascot** (who hides his pain with humor and provides the system with "comic relief").

All these roles are symptoms of the disease of **Co-Dependency**, in which the primary compulsion is to act in a manner which accommodates the Dependent. It is a primary, progressive and chronic disease that stands between the afflicted person and his ability to **act** from free choice rather than **react**, i.e., behave the way he learned in order to survive a sick situation.

On Monday, many people who were heretofore unfamiliar with my work come to terms with their own knowledge and feelings about co-dependency. They see themselves for the first time as people who experienced a painful family system and never left it emotionally. With their family issues "crystalized," they now have a hook into their own behavior patterns and feelings and something to work with over the next few days.

Tuesday morning, the psychodrama of "Reconstruction" (now "Restoration") begins. For the "Star," or person whose life we will be recreating all day and evening, the even began months before with his/her selection for that role. Once selected, the Star began amassing information about his family of origin, his grandparents' families, and the family in which he now lives. If he has done is job well, the Star will have a family tree, anecdotes and events of note securely in memory or on paper, snapshots, portraits, birth certificates, court records, adoption papers, and **a clear idea of his goals for the day.** For many of the Stars, this is a day of forgiveness, of letting go, of experiencing love they had forgotten they had, sadness they thought they had buried. This day will bring up many issues they did not think they had brought with them. And from this re-experiencing and re-feeling will come new healing.

I prepare for my work with the Star by interviewing him/her extensively just prior to the workshop itself. The purpose of the interview is twofold: First, I must know the person's life thoroughly, in order to guide them through it. I need a sense of where they are stuck in terms of old issues and what they are and are not willing to bring up before the group. Second, we need this time together in order to build the trust in each other that will make the journey a success.

Workshop participants are cast in specific roles in the Star's generational history. The casting process is mysterious, because many times the person cast is trying to deal with his/her own family issues inherent in that role. For example, if the Star is a man who casts me in the role of his daughter, I become a daughter again. This is one of the many roles I have played in my life, but I have not been a daughter to my father in many years. As I feel myself in this role, memories come flooding back. I go with my feelings, paying attention to the situation the Star wishes to recreate, and our dialogue flows. Together, we re-live an event from his past, and both of us learn that in that situation, each person did the best he could. A healing takes place, not just for the Star, but for the person so fortuitously cast in the role of daughter, who healed in **her** heart a breach with her own father. I do not know why this happens; I only know that the Star's life is a vehicle through which others can work.

These vignettes are re-enacted all day, punctuated with pauses as the group gives feedback on the various scenes. Participants may not analyze events; rather, they must concentrate on the feelings that come up. If they are strongly identifying with the incident being staged, I encourage them to work through their feelings in demonstrative ways: scream, move the anger up through the stomach and out the mouth. Take a bataca bat and beat past hurts and rage onto a pillow. Cry. If we **talk** about how we feel, we may come up with valuable insights; but the only way to work through feelings is to **feel.**

The drama moves in reverse. The Star's current family is examined first, followed by his life in his family of origin, and then his grandparents' families. Where the Star is today is not the result of random circumstance; he comes to view his life as the only one he could have had, given the generational path cut long ago.

A successful "Restoration" ends, not when the Star's work is done, but with the Star's awareness of where the work should begin. He now has choices, and he can make them freely and consciously.

Wednesday, the participants split into small groups for more individualized work. By this day, we have jelled into "family," and the small groups become very intimate. Those who surrender themselves to this feeling do the best work. In a loving, supportive atmosphere, the tears, rage, shame, pain, and ultimately the joy that people hide in order to live day-by-day come to the surface. It is, for many, the most exhausting and rewarding day of the workshop.

Thursday, we give a special party called **The Parts Party.** It is a Gestalt exercise in which one person lists his personal qualities, personifies them with well-known personalities, and casts one of the participants in each part. Then, as the "parts" sit down to a party with each other, the person walks the periphery of the "revelry," observing the interaction. Who dominates? Who brings the greatest joy? Who could best serve the party by leaving? As the person pauses next to each character, he may speak with them and negotiate terms under which they may stay. For example, the "comedian" at the party (often Rodney Dangerfield!), may stay if he does not dominate the loving, saintly Mother Therese! The Parts Party gives the "host" a chance to look at himself as the sum of his parts, to love parts of himelf without loving all, and conversely to reject some parts of himself without despairing that he is "all bad."

On that note, we end the workshop with the Serenity Prayer and cling to each other for must a moment longer. The four days are over, just when they should be, as many of the participants are anxious to go home and put into practice what they have experienced here. For me, I leave each "Restoration" Workshop with a profound respect for the people who have surrendered themselves to the process and gratitude to the Higher Power for leading me to this work.

The change in name of this workshop from "Reconstruction" to "Restoration," fills me with new eagerness to continue the work. **"Restoration"** connotates a desire to return people to their "original personhood," i.e., the person they were before they adapted their behavior to accommodate a sick system. And we seek to "restore" rather than to change. It is my greatest hope and wish that everyone with unsettled family issues will someday surrender themselves to "Family Restoration." And may it give each of you the same joy and hope it has given me.

Continuum of Care Essentials For Working with Families

By Nancy Whitaker Renaud and Peter Brown

The alcohol treatment field is gradually implementing a viable and consistent approach to the recovery process for the alcoholic. A continuum of care from Drunk Driver schools to Relapse Prevention has emerged over the last decade. However, just as concern for the family of the alcoholic has lagged behind than for the IP, so the development of a reliable format sequencing the treatment for a recovering family has been slow in coming. The rivalry between family therapists and alcohol counselors for the family treatment territory threatens to increase the delay in the availability of quality treatment.

Alcohol counselors who understand the disease are unfamilir with family system methods and are reluctant to address the problems of the non-alcoholic family members. Family therapists who treat the disease as a symptom of underlying systems problems, underestimate the power of the addiction and its chronic, progressive and irreversible effect on the addicted member.

It has become all too easy for the members of one professional group to ignore the expertise of the other which must be present for a lasting and successful recovery for every member of the alcoholic family. For recovery to be assured, the alcoholic family needs abstinence treatment, education about the disease, and family therapy. Moreover, it is not only the model of treatment that must be considered, but the appropriate timing for each integer. The continuum of care for the alcoholic family is divided into three distinct and separate stages.

First Stage

Recovery from any chronic illness requires treatment that addresses the physical aspect of the disease first. The goals of this treatment are to (a) keep the patient symptom-free and (b) to reduce flareups in duration and frequency. It is worse than useless to deal with the emotional or behavioral reactions to any chronic, irreversible, progressive disease while ignoring appropriate medical treatment to arrest the progress of the illness.

The fear a family has for the disease will always outweigh its need to get help and they will readily collude with the therapist who sees "Movement" as resolution. The first stage of treatment for family members can be accomplished prior to, or ideally, during the treatment the alcoholic experiences for his/her alcoholism. Many alcohol treatment programs already provide family intervention, education and support programs that are designed to assist families to recognize the assault the disease has made on their lives and to begin to survive without the alcohol focus. This cognitive and life-style refocusing forms the 'first step' in adequate family treatment.

Centered around abstinence from all psychoactive chemicals and an initial calming of the family system, the primary ingredient in this stage is the recognition and acceptance that the disease is a threat to the physical survival of a family member, and that the effect of living over a protracted period of time in the presence of the addiction has caused stress-related disorders in the other members of the family. Family work during early detoxification, withdrawal and post-acute withdrawal must be conducted in a manner similar to that used with the families of patients afflicted with other major disease—cancer, MS, heart disease. That is, groups should be educational concerning the disease, encourage the maintenance of good health, and be supportive with reference to such areas as (1) personal goals; (2) living with the disease; (3) behavior manifested in relation to the disease; (4) recovery and relapse; (5) grief and loss; and (6) resources and referral.

It is important during this stage of the recovery process to resist the temptation to over-repond to the family's obvious pain. Counselors who care and want to help, frequently expect too much, too fast from families. Treatment techniques that use assaultive confrontation tools to force quick change are all too likely to further the guilt and emotional separation already established within the family. Such methods at this stage of recovery may produce a sheen of "growth" that is only another form of unresolved depression. An understanding and acceptance of recovery as an ongoing process with highs and lows, slips and solid new growth, will be an assistance to both the counselor and the family. This knowledge encourages the "one-day-at-a-time," "first things first" integration of change and acknowledges that continuing recovery is a lifetime goal. An outline or chart of the recovery process, including family relapse prevention tools and a referral for continuing care with a family counseling center are helpful to assure that the family has the necessary back-up during the next stage of their recovery work.

Second Stage

The second stage of treatment can almost be called a "time out" from treatment. During this 9-18 month period, after abstinence treatment and education, a family needs the experience of "normalizing" without a specific treatment format. Therapeutic life experiences may continue in the form of friendships, membership in A.A., Al-Anon, ACoA, or Alateen, church attendance and educational settings. Treatment centers and counselors may be within telephone therapy reach, although an A.A. or Al-Anon sponser is probably a better and more cost-effective answer. A.A. and Al-Anon are particularly helpful during this stage of treatment, as they encourage the family to focus outward and to become involved in a socially-acceptable relationship with a safe therapeutic community.

During this first year of recovery, alcoholics and their families must create for themselves an environment that minimizes stress and that allows the family to experience life without continued crises. It is important the new stresses are not encouraged by support persons and that life events which might create problems be minimized. Alcoholic families may regress to old methods (drinking or drunk-like behavior) to handle stress if they have not had time to solidly establish new methods. Alcoholics Anonymous points out the need for low stress during early sobriety with the use of the acronym HALT, which was devised to remind recovering people that it is important not to get too Hungry, Angry, Lonely, or Tired. Alcoholic families must have time to get over their addiction to adrenalin.

Professionals who understand this concept support personal growth that is low stress-producing and delay issues that produce high anxiety.

"Time-out-of-treatment" also allows a needed interim for a return to optimum physical functioning. During the first twelve months of sobriety, the neuro-physiological recovery of the alcoholic is 50-80% accomplished. Cortical atrophy and central nervous system dysfunction are diminished. With this healing, the alcoholic will experience more clarity of thought and short-term memory will become more dependable.

Third Stage

The third stage of family treatment should not be addressed until stress-related disorders have declined and neurophysiological recovery has advanced. As this physical healing takes place, the family is more able as a group to face the unresolved issues that are the left-overs of the drinking years. Many marriages and many family groups do not survive recovery because of a failure to address their painful intimacy issues. Unattended to, these problems will solidify into permanently dysfunctional methods of dealing with interpersonal relationships. The opening-up of conflicts, the acquisition of new methods of communication and conflict resolution, and the experience of supportive interactions among family members are the agenda of this third phase of family treatment. This phase belongs to the arena of the experienced family therapist. Now is the time for the family members to expand their ability to handle stress without resorting to drinking or drunk-like behavior to reduce the anxiety and pain. During the drinking years, cues that once signaled closeness between family members come to be strongly associated with painful experiences. An obvious example of this confusion lies with the softening of facial muscles, glazing of eyes and blurring of focus that is noticed by partners and children as a significant sign of drunkenness and that may, in sobriety, be confused with similar responses during the emotional softening of intimate moments. Within the safe environment of the therapist's office, a family needs the opportunity to review its past, to confront its distrust and to come to amends with one another. Family history-taking can be an important tool during this process, encouraging a family to remember the varieties of its encounters and to come to a shared perception of its joint experience.

Hope for the expansion of our ability to deal effectively with the myriad of problems presented to us by alcoholic families lies in the joint effort of alcoholism treatment specialists and family therapy professionals learning to work with one another, and in the continuing interplay of learning between the two professions. It is not cost-effective to presume to train all alcohol counselors in the intricacies of family therapy, or to require family therapists to develop skills geared to detoxification or education about the disease process. However, it seems absolutely necessary that each profession understand and accept the primacy of the other within their arena and develop a willingness to refer to one another.

With continuing care, alcoholism may represent the chronic disease process from which a family has the potential to recover, with a significantly better relationship to all aspects of its life than they experienced prior to the disease.

The Role of Sexuality During Recovery and Active Chemical Dependence

By Gerald Shulman

It would be impossible to talk about the role of sexuality in recovery without relating it to the role of sexuality during the active chemical dependence, which impacts on both the chemically dependent person and family member (partner). The focus of this article will be primarily on alcohol, and other sedative-hypnotic drugs, because the scope is not sufficient to allow for a broader discussion of other drugs.

When looking at the impact of sexuality in recovery, major areas that need to be noted are sexual dysfunction, performance anxiety, self-image, past sexual behavior, communication, trust and intimacy. These individual areas are not discrete and may have a cumulative effect on current sexual adjustment and comfort. In this context, recovery is defined as total abstinence and an enhancement of functioning in every major area of a person's life (e.g., work, family, marriage, health, etc.), including self-image.

It is clearly documented that during active dependence, sexual dysfunction is most commonly a direct result of the depressant effects of the sedative/hypnotic drugs. However, during early recovery, chemically dependent people may be surprised by a continuation of the dysfunction because they may assume that the dysfunction is simply a result of being intoxicated. One common example is continued erectile difficulty in newly-recovering males because of a low testosterone level, which does not immediately rectify itself with sobriety. In both chemically dependent people and their partners, the history of past "failure" and the anxiety about performance may well be the major stumbling block to a relaxed and satisying sexual relationship, if not a functioning one.

In early recovery (less than six months), the recollection of dysfunction problems during the period of active dependence may well negatively affect current ability and interest in sex. The great emphasis placed on sexual performance in this culture, and its subsequent anxiety is further compounded with a recovering chemically dependent/co-dependent person, because of the history of dysfunction. The very anxiety about current functioning and the resultant "spectatoring" may become the major obstacle to effective functioning.

The self-image of both the chemically dependent person and partner almost always suffers during active addiction. In addition to the assault on one's value system that is a function of chemical dependence/co-dependence itself, some chemically dependent people and/or their partners may have engaged in sexual (e.g., extra-marital affairs, homosexual behavior, etc.), or no sexual behaviors (e.g., lying, verbal and physical abuse), which they now find unacceptable and which further negatively impacts on their self-esteem. They may feel unworthy and undeserving of a positive sexual relationship. The impact appears to be even more acute for female alcoholics for whom there is generally a greater stigma associated with alcoholism. Furthermore, many people (including the female alcoholic and male partner), may make some connection between female alcoholism and "sexual promiscuity."

Intimacy, communication and trust issues are very important, for both the recovering chemically dependent person and his/her partner. Such issues affect both the ability to function (e.g., potency, ability to orgasm), as well as those aspects of an adequate sexual relationship which are more than simply "equipment which functions."

Frequently, co-dependents have viewed sex as "awful" during the active dependence. If it is a wife, she has dealt with an alcoholic husband who has reeked of alcohol, who has ranged from less than a sensitive lover to brutal, and who may well have blamed his partner for all of his sexual problems. She (the partner), in turn may now feel guilty because she is not feeling aroused and responsive to this "sick alcoholic who is currently sober and going to meetings." Frequently, the partner believes that when the alcoholic gets sober, there should be an immediate ability on her (partner's) part to be warm, initmate and caring, and a corresponding ability by the newly-recovering alcoholic to immediately be able to perform flawlessly.

If the ability to communicate and trust has disappeared during the active addiction, it will take some time to redevelop. Sometimes it was not present even before the addiction, and therefore has to be established for the first time. The partner now is no longer able to place the responsiblity for his own sexuality and any sexual dysfunction onto the actively-using person ... can no longer blame the alcoholic. People have to share with one another what they really feel, in spite of their fears.

Trust issues and their relationship to intimacy and sexuality are further complicated by fears that the alcoholic may relapse or that now that the alcoholic is sober, she/he will leave the partner for someone more desirable. Given the high rate of divorce among recovering alcoholic couples, this fear is not totally without foundation. Commonly, there is residual anger that the family member has felt during the active addiction which blocks current feelings of intimacy.

Frequently, communication problems exist because there has not been a feeling language employed between the chemically dependent person and his/her partner. These communication problems, lack of trust, the residual anger, and a basic lack of interpersonal honesty which may have pre-dated or resulted from the dependence, become major obstacles to a satisfying relationship—sexual or otherwise. Looked at another way, the problems and the redevelopment of an adequate sexual relationship may be representative of the problems and the redevelopment of an overall relationship.

Unfortunately, in talking with many recovering chemically dependent people and partners who belong to A.A. and Al-Anon, the informal messages that they have received about sex are: (1) —

"you don't talk about it;" (2) you don't get involved for a year;" and (3) "it is equivalent to lust."

In the book *Twelve Steps and Twelve Traditions,* when talking about Step 4, it is suggested that as a means of avoiding confusion, a list be made of the "Seven Deadly Sins," one of which is lust ... what follows is a discussion about sex.

For those of us who have worked in the field and are aware of these admonitions which are provided to newly-recovering chemically dependent and significant others about sexuality, it is important that we reconsider them for accuracy, appropriateness and applicability. We are ethically bound to provide more appropriate suggestions.

"Don't get involved for one year!" What is magic about one year? Does the 365th day end at twelve midnight? If someone went to a residential program for treatment, is "one year" counted from the day of admission or the day of discharge? What is "involved?" A woman working in a halfway house confronted one of the residents who had recently visited a prostitute with the fact that he had breeched a house rule ... that of not "getting involved." His response was that he was not involved, it was simply a "business proposition." Is he not correct?

Newly recovering alcoholics and significant others frequently have very strong needs for intimacy. How can these be met in a safe and appropriate fashion? Can we not experience intimacy which is not sexual? The very sharing and caring that occurs in A.A. and Al-Anon and which makes them as effective as they are, speaks to intimacy.

One recommendation is to use a 4th Step Inventory, in part as a way of coming to know oneself sexually. In a regular inventory, the individual gains knowledge which should aid them to not repeat the behaviors that caused them to feel guilt and anxiety. Should not the same thing be said for knowing yourself sexually? What is acceptable sexual behavior for one person may not be acceptable for another. It may, in fact, be a threat to sobriety. People are not more identical in their sexual values than in any other way.

Historically, A.A. was not only considerably more conservative, but the people who joined A.A. were a much more homogenous group than today. This homogeneity was found in age, socio-economic level, drinking and drug use patterns, source of referral, stage of the illness, etc. At the very least, we are currently using some of the statements that may have been relevant 20 years ago on a population to which they are not nearly as meaningful today.

An analogy to sexuality issues and problems may be that of depression. Too frequently, alcoholics are diagnosed and treated as depressives because, in fact, they are depressed. In all probability, this depression is part of their disease of alcoholism. If the depression has not lifted after a period of recovery, then it must be re-evaluated because it may well be a separate affective disorder which does need attention. In a similar fashion, we can expect at least a disruption of sexual functioning, comfort levels, intimacy, and communication during addiction and in early recovery. However, assuming that the people involved are in recovery programs and they are making progress in other areas such as self-image, communication, etc., there should be progress in the area of sexuality at about the same rate. If not, it is then time for a more formal assessment and possible referral for treatment.

"Going to more meetings" is not a solution to sexual problems. "Therapy" may not be very threatening to many people in self-help groups. If the A.A. or Al-Anon member (although in my experience it would be more likely be the A.A. member), believes that his "Program" is the answer to all of his problems, then going into therapy may be perceived as a betrayal of A.A., or the indication that A.A. is not working. Obviously, this is not the case. If an alcoholic or significant other has an attack of appendicitis, the way to deal with it is not to go to more meetings.

Just as recovering chemically dependent people and their families can arrive at a place of greater adjustment, emotional health, and functioning than they ever did during or before the active dependence, there is no reason why this same thing cannot be true of their sexuality.

There are recovering people (both chemically dependent and co-dependent), who are obviously "turned on" with their lives and their recovery. There is no reason to believe that this same sort of enthusiasm is not possible and/or desirable relative to an individual's sexuality.

Family Violence

By Sharon Sweeney and L. John Key

Touching the lives of millions of Americans, family violence is now recognized as an urgent social problem. According to research (Steinmetz and Straus, 1973), an estimated 50-60% of the nation's 47 million couples have experienced at least one violent incident, and 10-25% suffer violence as a common occurrence. At least half of the women seeking divorces say they were beaten repeatedly during their marriages.

Various studies of wife battering indicate that about 85% of the men who batter and 30% of the women who are victims, grew up in violent homes (Gelles, 1974; Steinmetz and Straus, 1974; Walker, 1979).

Still other research on the roots of family violence shows that 80-90% of convicted felons in prison either were abused as children or grew up in homes where they witnessed violence. Further, 63% of the young men between ages 11 and 20 who are incarcerated in California prisons for homicide killed their mother's batterer.

The Research

To look at the causes, circumstances, and possible prevention of family violence, the Center for Abusive Behavior, a private practice in Pasadena, collected data for more than one year on a total of 44 batterers. They ranged in age from 21 to 67, with an average age of 35. The batterers came from different races, and a range of socio-economic classes and occupations. All but six were employed, and their occupations included postal carrier, certified public accountant, police officer, car wash employee, teacher, bartender, lawyer, engineer and minister. Of these men, 17 were referred by the probation department, and the rest were either self-referred or referred by community agencies. Half of the men had been abused as children, and 35% identified either their father, grandfather or brother as also being an abuser. Forty percent had a previous encounter with the criminal justice system for assaultive or other anti-social behavior. One-third were alcohol abusers.

There has not been any comprehensive research on this special population because, until recently, there were almost no counselors or agencies willing or equipped to treat the batterer. Therefore, the data base for the kind of man who beats his wife tends to come, not from the batterer himself, from from those involved as victims or helpers of the victims.

The batterer is described by the victim as having low self-esteem, denying and minimizing the degree and extent of the violence, demonstrating excessive possessiveness, jealousy and verbal abuse, and having traditional views of male and female role orientation. Further, the batterer generally has a history of being abused as a child himself.

From clinical interviews at the Center for Abusive Behavior, from the administration of a personality inventory questionnaire, and weekly summaries from "anger" diaries of the batterers, there is a recognizable constellation of attitudes, beliefs and emotional patterns common to those men who abuse their wives or have the potential to do so. Specifically, batterers tend to differ from the average male population on two personality characteristics. Batterers appear to be serious or sober and possibly dour and sometimes unimaginative. They are concerned about detail and are sometimes unimaginative. The majority have an external, rather than an internal locus of control orientation.

A Working Typology

The typology developed from the research suggested three subtypes of batterers: (1) Infrequent batterers (once every three or four months); (2) Frequent batterers (weekly); and (3) Mixed-type batterers (varying).

The infrequent batterer is rigidly inhibited by everything and everybody. He rarely responds with anger and aggression, no matter how great the provocation. Yet, he is unable to use the mechanics of displacement or response generalization and becomes abusive when his violent tendencies exceed his defenses.

The frequent batterers make up the majority of the batterers in the sample. They tend to respond with anger and aggression whenever frustrated.

Mixed-type batterers suffer some degree of frustration and their treatment may be as simple as identifying the source of frustration and learning new social skills.

In addition, all types of batterers tend to justify their abusive behavior by minimizing and denying the extent of the battering. (This is consistent with data collected by others). By minimizing the abuse, the batterer relieves himself of the responsibility of his behavior and the necessity of changing himself—also, by depression and suicidal thoughts.

This typology, based on our research, has its limitations, but it does offer a viable alternative to the practice of putting all batterers in one classification, treating them all the same, and believing that all abuse stems from the same stimulus.

For treatment procedures, it is crucial to know whether a batterer is a frequent or infrequent abuser. The frequent abuser needs to slow down and learn to not respond to stimuli which elicit aggression, whereas the infrequent batterer needs to be taught that he can respond appropriately to stimuli and not internalize his feelings and explode later. Also, if a client is on alcohol or drugs, he is encouraged to get detoxified and become actively involved in an Alcoholics Anonymous program before seeking help through this program for batterers.

The Therapeutic Alliance

As already pointed out, batteres tend to either deny, minimize or forget the violence they inflict upon their spouse. Further, batterers in general do not seek treatment of their own volition, but only upon the prodding of their wives or girlfriends, employers, clergy or the district attorney's office.

Upon entering treatment, the batterer often feels angrily justified in his hostile actions, defensive about his problem, and resistant toward therapy. It is difficult for him to give up a repertoire of behavior for which he has received intermittent reinforcement and about which he may feel pride. His environment is an American culture which rewards and values aggressive heroes and views violence as a problem solver. For all of these reasons, a therapeutic relationship is difficult to establish with most batterers.

To start to build a successful treatment relationship, however, a therapist must first deal with his or her own fears, anxieties, and repressed—or not so repressed—anger, brought about by the client's hostility toward treatment and potential for acting out, aggressive impulses. The fears and anxiety of the therapist can activate countertransference feelings that can interfere with the neutrality needed for a therapeutic alliance. Fear, in fact, may permeate the setting to such an extent that effective psychological intervention becomes impossible.

To avoid that situation, the therapist must take a constructive, non-judgmental stance at the beginning of the interview. The therapist must be non-judgmental toward the batterer as a person, yet judgmental about his abusive behavior and the effects of that behavior on the victim. The batterer must be reminded that he is responsible for his own behavior, yet, at the same time, encouraged and supported as he attempts to assume this responsibility. A successful therapeutic relationship can help a client realize, perhaps for the first time in his life, that he can control his anger and impulsive behavior.

The treatment approach that follows is applicable to male batterers with histories of frequent or infrequent batterings. While the sample was small, the current follow-up data suggest the positive potential for broad-based behavioral change. It is, obviously, of paramount importance that the batterer receive treatment for his behavior, since 40-60% of women are returning to violent relationships whether or not the batterer is in treatment.

Initial assessment

During the first session, according to the model used by the Center for Abusive Behavior, the therapist inquires about the most recent occurrence of assaultive behavior and listens for clues that indicate the violent style of the client and the factors that trigger abusive behavior. What are the physiological indicators that let the client know he is about to become physical? Does he, for example, clinch his fists, grit his teeth, get red in the face, or feel his stomach turn as he becomes angry? What is the frequency of these triggering behaviors? What is the duration of the anger? How often do the initial signs of anger become intense enough to cause physical assaults? What are the circumstances surrounding the anger and battering—money crises, alcohol problems or family pressures? Finally, in what environments does the batterer demonstrate impulse control problems—at work, social events, the home?

After the initial session, the client is asked to complete an "anger" diary of each incident of anger that he experiences during the week. The diary should focus on the circumstances that trigger the anger, the intensity and duration of the anger, the thoughts that the client has while angry, and the physiological signs of the anger, because feelings register in the body much sooner than in the head or the brain. The client can be taught to cue into the physical signs of his anger—muscle tension, aggressive feelings, etc.—so he can use the cues as an early warning system for himself and others. The cue, or signal, can be relayed either verbally or non-verbally. The batterer can learn to say, "I am too angry now to talk," or he can use a time-out signal to alert the spouse. The victim must mutually agree to this tactic and realize that the client must immediately leave the angry situation to avoid a violent confrontation.

The client must also learn to listen to what he says to himself before, during, and after an anger situation. This silent monologue has been labeled "negative self-talk" by Albert Ellis, the founder of rational-emotive therapy, and by Aaron Beck, the developer of cognitive treatment of depression.

The anger-producing negative self-talk usually takes the form of: "That bitch, who the hell does she think she is, telling me what to do?" or: "I can't take it, she has gone too far." Once the client begins to listen to the statements he is making to himself, he can be taught to develop positive statements, on 3x5 cards, to contradict the negative statements. Such positive self-talk statements may include the following: "I can control myself. I'm the only one who can control myself. I don't need to prove anything." The purpose of these statements is to get the client to understand that he has feelings other than anger.

In summary, in the initial phase of treatment, the therapist should have the client tune into his physiological signs of anger, use his time-out signals, perform deep breathing exercises or progressive relaxation techniques, and then read silently his positive self-talk statements. The goal of each of these steps is to ultimately pair relaxation with physiological arousal.

The Middle Phase

Because the violence can potentially be stopped within a short period of time, most abusers or batterers attempt to—and sometimes do—discontinue treatment after one to seven sessions. However, as Ganley et al. (1978) point out, the batterer is at risk for the rest of his life and should be encouraged to continue treatment for at least six months to a year. In the model used at the Center for Abusive Behavior, the client is encouraged to become more thoroughly acquainted with his abusive or battering self through a variety of therapeutic teaching techniques such as transactional analysis, projective drawing and the egogram as developed by Dusay (1977). Dusay defines the egogram as a visual symbol that represents the total personality of any human being, by separating it into its various aspects and clearly showing which parts are "weak" and which parts are "strong."

As further steps in the middle phase of treatment, the client's "anger" behavior is monitored from week to week. The client's spouse is spoken to frequently by telephone, and is periodically invited to therapy sessions. In addition, the Center offers a "male role group" which focuses on male/female defined roles and the way in which these characteristics apply to, or interfere with, present or past relationships. Also, there is a continuing attempt to teach assertion training techniques and non-violent conflict resolution.

The Third Phase

Women who have been battered or are being battered also need specialized counseling. They may not psychologically understand battering and its effects, and they may be indecisive about whether to stay with their partner.

The client usually begins by discussing her "war stories" about the violence in her home. After that catharsis, the client is ready to listen and learn about the battering syndrome. The therapist should inform her about the shelters available, and the fact that unless something is done about the problem, the violence will get worse. Above all, she should be made aware that the violence is not a result of what she has done, but that the batterer is responsible for his lack of impulse control and violent actions. She must understand that assault is a crime and is not to be condoned.

The woman client who has been beaten over a long period of time often has a low level of self-esteem about her role as wife, lover or mother. Often, she believes implicitly what the partner has been telling her. Also, a woman who has been verbally and physically abused begins to fight back. She needs to look at her problems with impulse control and her desire to win an argument or have the last word. The therapist can help her examine the fights and gain perspective and insight into her relationship and the behaviors surrounding it.

As the relationship between the therapist and the battered woman grows, the client may or may not leave the violent situation. Still, she can monitor the fights and become aware of options other than fighting. Some women, even after leaving a battering situation, remain in therapy to insure that they won't repeat the violent pattern again.

The children in the abusive family have been affected by seeing or experiencing the violence and need to be evaluated and treated professionally. They need to understand that the parents are not fighting because of anything that they did and that they cannot control the fighting.

Art therapy and play therapy are effective tools for bringing out the child's feelings and thoughts. Through drawings, puppets and dolls, the child can represent his family involved in typical scenes of conflict. Then, the child can be encouraged to consider options other than fighting. By this technique, the child can learn ways to step away from the destructive behavior.

After the individual counseling for the wife and children is terminated, and the abusive behavior has stopped, conjoint therapy may be initiated, if desired.

In the initial stage of conjoint therapy, the couple must learn basic communication skills. They need to understand how to be a sender and a receiver of communication from their spouse. They are encouraged not to engage in name-calling or to bring up problems or grievances more than 48 hours old which tend to cloud the main issue.

Through treatment, the couple learns to monitor their arguments and give signals to each other to avoid a physical confrontation. They are encouraged to bring their disagreements into the therapy session, rather than to fight them out at home. With treatment, they understand that through negotiation and re-education, they can learn to lead a better married life without physical violence.

Summary

In addition to therapeutic techniques, successful treatment depends to a great extent on the attitude and skills of the therapist. In deciding whether to work with batterers as a treatment population, the therapist must be aware of his or her own skills with anger management and fears about violence.

An ability to maintain a supportive relationship and to work through angry crises is essential. Since the therapist will be teaching the client basic skills in anger management and relaxation, he or she must be able to successfully combine teaching with the therapeutic process. With appropriate skills and attitudes, therapists can effectively help motivated batterers control their anger and impulsive behavior.

Family Aftercare: An Ongoing Process

By Andrea Dennison & Jane Hathaway

Initially, it seemed somewhat curious that a presentation on family treatment was being given by a family therapist **and** an Aftercare director. However, upon further thought, we realized the opportunity was more by design, rather than serendipitious. It reflected the natural outcome of growth and integration of the family treatment process at Spofford Hall.

At its inception, Spofford Hall's family treatment program was a discrete unit with a separate staff and schedule. Interaction between family patients and chemically dependent patients was limited and tightly scheduled. As we became more aware of the similarities between chemical dependence and co-dependence, we began to blur the boundaries between the programs, pirating pieces from each to create an environment conducive to the healing of whole families.

We began to share treatment planning time and office space with the staff of the 28-day program. A great deal of cross-training occurred. We recognized chemical dependence sooner in our family patients, and family of origin issues earlier in our chemically dependent patients. In preparing for our workshop, we hoped that people would come away with the family treatment process demystified: **treating affected family members is like treating chemically dependent people.** Once past detoxification, alcoholism treatment addresses denial, delusion, obsession, compulsion, low self-esteem and a reservoir of avoided feelings.

We provide detoxification for family patients as well. Feelings of confusion and numbness in the family patient can be likened to chemical withdrawal as family members are brought face-to-face with their addiction to their significant addict. It is important for those patients to learn that their relationship with a person closely resembles the other person's relationship with a drug. A graphic representation of this is the "identical symptoms" exercise, used by Spofford's family treatment staff during the weekly One-Day Program.

Education and Intervention

The One-Day Program is offered weekly, on visiting day, to families and friends of chemically dependent people, and as a community service. It is required that family members of the chemically dependent patients attend at least once while their loved one is in treatment. Its purpose is two-fold: education and intervention.

The format consists of an overview of treatment at this facility, question and answer sessions, and communication exercises designed to help co-dependents focus on themselves, their disease, and their recovery needs.

To achieve this end, we often use the following exercise:

Visitors are asked to help the group facilitators compile a list of the symptoms of drug and alcohol dependence. They are asked to do so in behavioral terms: "What do you see?" "What does it look like?" Responses are listed on a blackboard in the front of the classroom and often number fifty different symptoms.

Amid much groaning, the board is erased and participants are simply asked, "What is it like for you?" Responses are slow at first, but as the group gives itself permission to speak, a whole new, nearly identical list is generated. This leads to discussion of the disease concept and the fact that no diagnosis is based on only one symptom; that if chemical intake is disregarded for the moment, both groups have exactly the same symptoms. The facilitator is then able to talk about alcoholism and co-alcoholism within the same framework.

The program then moves on to a showing of the "Family Trap," Sharon Wegscheider's film about chemically dependent families, followed by a discussion of family roles and symptoms. The symptoms are real and personal, having just been generated by the group. The presentation of survival roles has a powerful impact on the audience as they gain, often for the first time, a name for what they have been feeling and doing for much of their lives. This recognition provides them with the hope for recovery.

Experiential Approach Necessary

Our approach to family treatment is largely experiential in nature.

Talk therapy readily lends itself to the triangulated style of communications, so dangerous and so familiar to the members of the alcoholic family. Instead of "When he said _____, I felt _____," so common in most talk therapies, "when you said _____," I felt _____," within the context of a roleplay, group or sculpture gives the patient some practical communication skills. This is important for two reasons.

Insight alone can be dangerous to the co-alcoholic who intellectualizes, allowing continued avoidance of painful feelings. Additionally, people from alcoholic families have lived for years in a web of lies and delusion. Words have been used primarily for alibis and blaming, so patients are often unable to distinguish "helping words" from "hurting words." Turning aspects of recovery into experiences which are visible and tangible gives them credibility. Seeing and feeling recovery are first steps: treatment should next be structured to provide repeated opportunities to use new coping skills.

Frequently, we encounter patients with very sophisticated denial systems, who pass quickly from simple denial to a more complex form that involves play-acting and compliance. The "right" experience may tell the patient in a way words can't. For example, he may need to rely on his group to get his dinner for him, in order to talk about what it feels like to be out of control.

There are times when discussion of experiential approaches sounds like "anything goes." This is far from the truth. It is important to be aware of the patient's emotional response patterns and perceptions ... and to know what experience one is trying to create for the patient. A literal approach often works, e.g., someone who is "holding on to the resentments" needs something to hold on to, a dependent persons needs someone or something to lean on. This can often be accomplished by use of a family sculpture.

Family Sculpture: Experiential Tools

Very simply, sculpting is the process of arranging people in postures, locations or poses that best represent the emotional relationships of the family or patient involved.

The patient must be able to describe people involved ... feeling words are useful. It is then up to the therapist to have a "bag of tricks" to represent, in three dimensions, the emotions and relationships being explored.

The rules set for other group members are simple. Interpretation is not allowed.

Sculptures may be stationary or may evolve into role plays. They may be silent or the therapist may ask the role players to share what they are feeling within the context of the role that they play.

The staff may devise a sculpture to bring feelings to the surface. Patients are supported in expression of their anger and fear, and encouraged to identify defenses they employed in the past. They may then be given the opportunity to say some of the things they "wish they could have said at the time." By this time, the transference may be strong enough so that giving the patient control of the sculpture proves fruitful. The patient may demand or insist that the others either leave the room, apologize, or hug him. Patients intuitively "finish" the sculpture in the way that they need.

Talk therapy has its place in sewing up experiences for people. For example, the patient who ends her sculpture by receiving a hug from her violent relative must acknowledge that this might not happen. It then becomes the therapist's role to extract something the patient can "keep" from the sculpture. Can she verablize the belief that she doesn't deserve to be beaten?

Sculpting is a technique that is used in group setting, to help patients make an emotional connection with some of their mental imagery or symbolism. Often, by describing the people with whom they have relationships, the group therapist is able to pose members of the group in positions that represent power, dominance, victimization, powerlessness and fear in one another's lives. A patient frequently bases his decisions on another person's actions, but refuses to call it anything but "considerate." That person is placed at the feet of the decision-maker, both emotionally and dynamically. Literally placing one person at another's feet, either by seating one on the floor or standing the other on a chair creates the same strain physically as the relationship does emotionally.

The Set and The Setting

A residential environment is safe and can be manipulated to yield far more than education. Examination of the rules and surroundings, through a lens of free-association can offer a variety of symobols recreating "real-life" issues and events. It is important not to get carried away with the potential fun or whimsy of some of the exercises and continually check back to see how the patient is interpreting things.

We work with a set of attitudes that provide a safe framework for the beginning of recovery. The first is that chemical and co-dependence are diseases of feelings. Many people enter treatment with terrifying fantasies about what will happen if they express their emotions. Treatment provides them with the knowledge that they can verbalize their feelings.

It is expected that patients in the family treatment program take every opportunity to verbalize their feelings. It is through this repetition that they become able to break their personal cycles of repression. The treatment team provides a role model for patients with their relaxed approach to the expression of feelings.

While patients are learning to express their feelings, they are provided with two rules: no triangulation (i.e., speak to the person you are talking about), and make "I" statements. The use of "I" statements keeps the family member focused on him/herself, doesn't allow him/her to hide in group opinions, and enables him/her to begin to take risks.

Summary

As patients receive information, they identify painful experiences in their own histories. As they attempt to express that pain they may cry, yell, or voice a desire to "hit something."

At those times, it is particularly important for staff to convey their acceptance of the patient and all of his/her feelings. Also, staff must show their belief in patients' recovery potential and knowledge that patients possess the capacity to do things they have not yet tried: mourning, asserting, celebrating. A significant step toward recovery is taken when patients are able to implement behavior changes.

Patients may not always be able to talk about their gains or changes in self-perception. They don't need to when their behavior reflects them.

Breaking Through the Family's Denial

By Dene Stamas, M.A., C.A.C.

Although the effect of alcoholism within the family is a relatively new area of research and study, it is quickly becoming obvious that the family, as well as the alcoholic, needs help in order to facilitate the recovery process.

Just as denial is the first barrier to be removed in treating the alcoholic, so it is with the family. Members are defending against the same Pandora's box of feelings as the alcoholic's anxiety, anger, guilt, remorse, and pain. The tend to over-react or under-react to situations and their behavior can become as inconsistent and confusing as the alcoholic's!

Denial is what helps prevent people from feeling pain or looking at a difficult situation. Denial helps illnesses and problems to continue to grow. An analogy to denial is novocaine, usually given by the dentist to prevent pain. Let's imagine that a person who has a cavity goes to the dentist, who would give the patient some medication to take away the pain, without treating the cavity. The cavity or decay continues to progress, and the pain becomes more severe. Denial is usually our way of dealing with pain, which most of the time is self-defeating.

It is my belief that denial needs to be broken, so that the person knows he is hurting, and begins to learn that he can change and find more effective solutions. (If you don't change, everything remains the same!)

The major fuel for denial is resentment (which is fermented anger). If anger is not addressed, the wall of denial continues to grow. Once the anger has been lifted, the hurt of pain appears. If the hurt is not processed and dealt with effectively, the layer of anger will re-appear, followed by denial.

Some counselors feel that breaking through denial is like breaking in a horse. Once it is broken, it is broken. Unfortunately, denial can, and usually does, struggle to reappear, so counselors need to be aware and keep their eyes and ears open.

Another very important concept in helping the family is that they must learn to separate the drinking behavior from the drinker; to view the alcohol as the villain—not the alcoholic. Family members should also understand that their reaction to the alcoholism gives them too few choices as to who they are and what they would like to be. Each family needs to realize that many of the behaviors and attitudes are learned unconsciously, in trying to survive in an alcoholic family, and may not be what they want. In many ways, the family members have masks because of the alcoholism. Behinds the masks are questions like: "Who am I really?"; "Would you still like me if you really knew me?"; "Why can't I just be me?" These and other attitudes contribute to their lives being likened to a record that continues to repeat itself. You hear the same old things over and over again.

There are many techniques to break through denial, and I will endeavor to briefly describe 12 of them.

Generalization

The counselor make statements which are broad enough to teach everyone in the family, yet specific enough to zero in on a particular problem or need. Statements such as: "Many times the members of the alcoholic family find it difficult to really know who they are, or ask themselves questions like "Why do I feel so guilty when I'm having fun?" Other times, I would use generalizations to start a session with a group of alcoholics.

Generalizations help to set the tone, and start the family members looking at themselves individually. Generalizations also contribute to reducing denial and breaking down the family's reluctance to look at the problem.

Disclosure

The family is asked to share specific information with each other, to give everyone a chance to disclose his/her point of view.

Some specifics would be (Use only one example per family session):

1. What they like and what they dislike about themselves;
2. My most embarrassing situation;
3. The happiest time in my life;
4. The time I felt all alone.

The only rule is that everyone shares, without being interrupted by questions, followed by processing of the information shared.

Sometimes **Disclosure** is used as a family confrontation, where each family member shares specific information with the alcoholic on how his/her drinking has hurt them. I feel that recollections of what they liked about Mom or Dad (if Mom or Dad are the alcoholics), should be shared also.

Ventilation of Anger

Often times anger suddenly surfaces as defenses and denial decrease. Typically, there is a lot of anger in the family which has built up over a long period of time. Early in the sessions it is desirable to employ this particular technique. This ventilation will prevent crippling resentments and the attitude "I'm O.K.—He's got the problem." While resentments remain high, denial remains high.

Magnify the Pain of Being An Alcoholic Family

This is used to enable the family to look at how destructive alcoholism has been in their lives, and how it hurts every member. One of the best ways to magnify the pain is to **exaggerate the uglies** of being in an alcoholic family. One example of this is to have the alcoholic share the worst even that ever happened to him/her. One of my patients shared that she had left her two-year-old son alone in their apartment while she went out to buy more alcohol. When she came back, the building was on fire. Her son was all right, as she explained the fire had started on the top floor, but her apartment was on the first floor which was not affected. As she related this worst happening, she talked very fast and appeared to be little affected by what had happened. I magnified the situation by having her repeat it again, only this time in a much slower fashion. I also asked for other details, like what kind of a day it was, who else was around, etc. The more details that are shared, the more the person feels the situation. I also added that her drinking behavior, not **her real self**, could have killed her son. The purpose is to have her see how alcohol is hurting her and that it (alcohol) is a potential killer—not her.

Switching Roles

This technique allows the alcoholic family to experience a problem in a different light and from another point of view. A significant person in the alcoholic's life or the family member's life is chosen, and the subject is to assume their identity and respond as that person.

Sharing an Experience

With a particular person or family member in mind, the counselor shares a story which deals with a specific problem with a moral attached to it. The moral of the story is designed to encourage a new behavior or a new attitude.

Advantages and Disadvantages

It is very important for family members to look at the advantages and disadvantages of being in an alcoholic family. The counselor may start by having each family member share one advantage of mom or dad's drinking. One response has been: "Well, Dad, when you were drinking I could get away with murder, and you wouldn't put me through the third degree as to where I had been, or what time I came home." After every member shares the advantages, the counselor then asks each family member to share the disadvantages.

Indirect Awareness

Many times as a counselor confronts a specific family member, his/her defenses become high. The families will often distort important information. To address this problem the counselor directs the information to one family member with a specific message, which is actually intended for another member. It is amazing how the intended family member is very receptive to the information when it is not directed at him.

Last Time Technique

To help family members be specific and to reveal important information about their family illness, the counselor starts the session by informing the family that the illness of alcoholism has affected every member, and it is important to share their personal experiences. The counselor then asks the family members to recall certain experiences by completing such statesments as: "The last time I cried ..."; or, "The last time I thought I was going crazy ..."; or "The last time I had fun ...;" or "The last time I was depressed ..."; or, "The last time I felt all alone ..."; and, "The last time I was angry ..." This technique helps prevent internalization of thoughts and feelings, and gives the family a way to communicate and ventilate their pain.

A Rating on a Scale of 1 to 10

This technique is used to facilitate the family group to evaluate each other as to the degree of denial, truth, disclosure and honesty. A family member is asked to recall a certain time which is very specific and painful. The family then gives feedback on what has been shared, rating it on a scale from 1 (very shallow) to 10 (very deep). Many times, you can find high denial in the rater, who will rate a 10 for a response that the group, on an average, rated 4-5.

Paradoxical Approach

This approach works exceptionally well with rebellious family members. Ask the family not to do what you want them to do. Most rebellious people have an unwritten rule, "I will do the opposite of what you tell me to do or not do." Knowing this, you may say, "I don't want you to think about how you have been affected by your brother's alcoholism."

Planting Seeds

This is very valuable when a counselor wishes a family member to think about a certain subject, or share a specific incident. Sometimes a family member may say, "I'm a good listener and I prefer just to listen," or they may say very little and appear scared and shy. It is very important to pace your families while setting up certain expectations within certain time frames.

Many times, when the family member is not pushed, s/he will feel comfortable and open to talk much sooner. In other words, plant your seeds today and tomorrow watch them grow!

These techniques are but a few examples of the ways in which a counselor may break through denial. However, it must be remembered that all the techniques available will not be as effective if the counselor does not take the time to create an atmosphere which is comfortable and as free from anxiety as possible.

Above all, use humor. A good laugh or even a smile does more to relieve anxiety and create a therapeutic atmosphere than almost anything else.

Grief & Loss—Constant In Alcoholic Families

By John O. Neikirk

In my 10 years in the chemical dependency field, I have heard many explanations of alcoholism and the family. The philosophies differ, depending on whom you ask: clergy, self-help groups, psychotherapists, family systems therapists, or treatment center counselors. One attempt at understanding the chemically dependent family which seems to draw from all disciplines is that of loss and grief. This approach appears to draw consensus from the various helping professionals.

In my own counseling with families, there have always been nods of recognition when the subject of loss is brought up. Surprisingly, a tremendous gap exists in the professional literature on the combined subject of grief and chemical dependency. There has been much written on each separately, but a recent literature search spanning tens of thousands of articles only produced seven items on the the two subjects together. The following article is a beginning attempt to bridge the two areas: to talk about the kinds of losses a chemically dependent family faces, how they react to them, and implications for treatment and recovery. It is this article's premise that working with family members in terms of their loss and grief will help therapists maintain a non-judgmental and caring framework.

Types of Loss

The family involved with chemical dependency experiences more and more loss as the illness progresses. Personal serenity is lost to worry and fear. Self-esteem erodes into guilt and self-doubt. Where bonds of emotional trust and safety once existed, there remains suspicion and abused vulnerability. Social activities with friends and relatives gradually disappear as family isolation and embarrassment build. Significant loss occurs in predictability of life style. Families talk about not being able to count on regular meals, income, communication, emotional responses, or bodily safety. There is further loss of physical health—sleep disturbances, weight fluctuations, headaches, backaches, bruises, muscle spasms, ulcers, colitis, and more. Family members increasingly find themselves in hospitals and institutions, thus physically away from home and the familiar. Loss also occurs when young children run away, adolescents move out of the home prematurely, and divorce dissolves the marriage. Finally, there are the losses within the spiritual dimension. What used to give life meaning no longer is as significant or supportive. Old familiar values are assaulted by upsetting behaviors leaving each family member more bewildered and estranged. Sadly, this spiritual void results more often than we can know in another type of loss, that of death and suicide.

It is with these kinds of losses that chemically dependent families struggle. Nearly all individual and family dynamics connected with alcoholism can be viewed in terms of an ever-increasing set of losses. What happens to a family when faced with such challenges? Much has been written on how people react to and cope with the stress of loss.

Reactions to Loss

Perhaps the two most prominent authorities on loss are Erich Lindemann and Elisabeth Kubler-Ross, two psychiatrists who devoted their life work to helping people with grief and loss. In my opinion, their greatest contribution was to let people know that is it normal and natural to have painful and upsetting reactions during a grieving period. My job as a therapist also is to let chemically dependent families know the same, and to give them an opportunity to better understand, grieve, and accept their losses. Regardless of theoretical bias and academic training, this is generally what all helpers do when working with alcoholic families—allow them to acknowledge and accept the reality of their situation, which is one of great loss. From this knowledge and acceptance can come change.

Lindemann's work focused on loss through death. He was the first (1944) to see common reactions to acute loss. The parallels with the alcoholic family are striking. Lindemann wrote about the intense preoccupation with the deceased the survivors exhibited. Chemical dependency counselors see the same strong preoccupation with the alcoholic on the part of certain family members (the joke about the wife responding "He's fine" to a friend's inquiry on how her day was going). Lindemann saw families of dead people feel extremely guilty that somehow they caused or could have prevented death. "If only I hadn't let him drive on New Year's Eve." Alcoholic families wrestle with the same guilt. "I know she is addicted because I'm not a loving marriage partner." Lindemann noticed a pattern of anger over a death. "It's your fault she died" is said to spouses, relatives, doctors, hospitals, and to God. Chemical dependency self-help groups warn new members that blame and resentments are character defects that block recovery and serenity. Therapists often hear family members enraged about "why does this have to happen to me!"

Lindemann noticed that acute grief over death frequently produced somatic complaints and disease. It has been mentioned earlier in this article that family members of alcoholics also translate their stress and loss into physical symptomatology. A corporate leader in understanding this somatic component in family members in the work force is the Kemper Insurance Company of Long Grove, Illinois. Statistics about family physical problems can be gotten by writing to their Personal Assistance Program. Lindemann documented frequent occurrences of over-activity as the way to cope with loss; and children and spouse "co-dependency" groups often find this phenomenon present with alcoholic family members—the inability to relax and slow down. Finally, a commonality shared by Lindemann's findings, as well as the chemical dependency profession, is that family members frequently struggle with low self-worth involved with the losses. I've heard counselors say to a family member that from the way others speak about him that they must think he is nothing but garbage. The unfortunate response, way too often, is that the individual sadly agrees.

Kubler-Ross mentions some of the above characteristics in her work with dying patients, and also focuses on denial and bargaining, two additional aspects frequently observed in alcoholic families as well. The dying patient refuses to believe the prognosis of death. Similarly, the family member of the alcoholic will sometimes deny the existence of alcoholism, or his/her part in it. The dying patient will often bargain in coming to grips with his condition ("Please let me have one more Christmas"), and the family member involved with chemical dependency also will try to strike a deal with the alcoholic, with the treatment center, or with God ("You get my husband sober and then I will get help for myself").

One can see the striking parallels betwen research findings in the traditional grief literature and those observations with chemically dependent families. There is no doubt that these families experience the same loss dynamics and grief reactions that are encountered with more traditional death and dying situations.

Treatment and Recovery

What we find in general with all the above reactions is that the family member is fighting against the various losses, attempting to control an unmanageable situation—the progression of active chemical dependency. Their attempt to control the alcoholic is the very thing which produces more loss (of serenity, of self-worth, health, emotional closeness). Both Lindemann and Kubler-Ross were correct in saying that the solution to grief is to accept the loss. The family member must learn to accept the losses involved with alcoholism and only then will he/she find serenity and the ability to get on with life. Family members whom I have counseled often say that they long for the way things were before active chemical dependency. That can never be, and their serenity depends upon accepting the new reality.

To accept loss, the family member must first admit that the losses have taken place and that they are powerless to change anyone else except themselves. A therapist's job is to help remove the blocks to the natural grieving process. Some of these blocks may be denial, fear, pride, guilt, depression, anger, and not having a feeling language with which to express oneself. Family members must feel safe to be able to grieve, for to do so is very painful. Yet it is a natural process which leads to healing. The therapist can help by inviting (not demanding) that the family member talk about the losses. Blocks will disappear as the family member is able to identify and experience these blocks. This requires courage, not only of the client, but also of the therapist, to be truly present to someone else's pain (whether in the form of tears or anger), is not easy, and it is the mark of an experienced therapist who can allow the person to fully experience their grief. Inexperienced counselors stop this process prematurely, often due to their own anxiety. In the experiencing comes the healing, for grieving is a healthy process. Ultimately, relief comes when we realize that we are not able to control, to play God, to be all-powerful. People will fight for any other reason to explain their powerlessness, other than to admit that they are not God. One reason they use is to say, "I'm no good (lack of self-worth). This self-esteem returns when the person accepts his/her losses, the ultimate one being that he/she is not all-powerful and able to control others.

Over the years I have noticed that some counselors working with chemically-dependent families become frustrated, impatient, and overly confrontive with their clients. They begin to lose their compassion. I have found that reframing the situation in terms of grief and loss helps to restore the counselor's compassion and ability to be non-judgmental. The reframing also provides some therapeutic direction for both family and therapist. The family is in the midst of experiencing multiple deaths. Their behaviors and feelings are in direct response to these deaths. Helping professionals can assist by understanding and encouraging these families through their vulnerable grieving period. The precious goal of serenity awaits those who are able to move through their grief to ultimately accepting their losses.

Nutrition & Dysfunctional Families

By Sandra Cohen-Holmes, M.Ed., and Donald R. Land, Ph.D.

The multiplicity of problems generated by alcoholism in a family requires an approach that can meet head on the distorted thinking patterns and perceptions, difficulties with feelings and the race against time that many family members experience in their attempts to recover.

Our purpose is to present a model of behavior and treatment strategy which combines elements of psychonutrition, stress management, family systems and communication. The central hypothesis in this model is that biological and nutritional integrity is fundamental to the development of effective living skills, positive self-image, and meaningful relationships.

This approach includes tangible health and wellness-promoting activities that are supportive of the balanced thinking and healthy brain functioning necessary for recovery, effective living, and healthy interactions. These activities must be **do**-able by each family member and must be seen by each member as supportive of the overall health of the entire family.

Alcoholics, spouses, and especially adult children of alcoholics are up against the clock, trying to catch up to and learn the social and emotional skills that will allow them to feel the confidence and self-esteem so lacking or destroyed by their contact with this disease. Proper diet and nutrition provide new raw materials that can fuel and accelerate recovery, and provide the building blocks for a new body and mind. These raw materials will increase their chances for clear thinking, congruent feelings, emotional stability, and effective individual and interpersonal behaviors.

The Well-Fed Brain

The brain is more dependent upon the raw materials of optimum diet and nutrition than is any other part of the body. Food with which one fuels and builds the brain has a great deal to do with the quality of one's perception, thinking, feeling, behavior and consciousness. The symptoms of a malnourished or toxic brain are, in many ways, identical to symptoms of alcoholism in a family. These symptoms limit one's abilty to think clearly, to have accurate memory of past events and actions, to be aware of the consequences of actions, to perceive reality, to evaluate, to make clear decisions and maintain emotional balance, all of which are necessary for recovery from alcoholism and its effects. Resulting difficulties in thinking and behavior include: mood swings, unpredictable behavior, irrational beliefs, limited perspectives, negative thinking, fear-provoking fantasies, and difficulties with identifying and expressing feelings that lead to gross interpersonal communication problems.

The Raw Material of Recovery

Just as a better fuel to the brain provides for better thinking and behavior, better thinking and behavior also lead to healthier lifestyle and food choices, creating an upward spiral of improvement. When this fuel consists of life, freshness and a sense of value, one's thinking begins to take on the same characteristics. The newness and freshness of one's total intake—feelings, thoughts, ideas and food—helps to build the consciousness that is necessary to support new beginnings, new development and repairing of old ways. Thus, food represents not only actual live, fresh input, but is a metaphor for a new, fresh life.

Making healthy food

In addition to the direct nutritional benefits of healthy foods, there are social benefits. Many alcoholic families have to combat a long history of stress associated with mealtimes. Restructuring this significant aspect of family life into a safe, consistent and positive family experience is a move toward giving individuals the power of making choices and taking action toward their own healing and the health and unity of the family as a whole.

Making healthy meals together can be a bonding, centering, and supportive activity for a recovering alcoholic family. As a multi-faceted activity, it focuses on both prevention and treatment. Its many facets include social skillbuilding and cooperation in a process that is, in part, nonverbal and relatively non-threatening. It gives a family concrete materials and a process about which to communicate, cooperate, interact and learn together. Working toward the common goal of eating together and building confidence by building small successes around each meal is involving of all family members, regardless of age, experience or level of recovery.

Better Nutrition is Better Thinking, Feeling & Acting

The link between nutrition and recovery is seen most explicitly in one's ability to carry out the intellectual activities necessary to be alert and focus on recovery. To obtain the benefits of recovery through self help support groups in inpatient or outpatient settings, individuals with damaged feelings and difficulties with thinking and perception need an **accurate memory** and the ability to **challenge** intellectually their "picture" of reality. They must be able to **recognize** that they have choices and **choose** to act on those choices.

Alcoholic family members, as a result of mental misperception, cannot trust their own thinking. Distorted thinking, misperception of reality, fantasizing, focusing on the past, fear focusing on the future, obsession on an event or person, can create out-of-control thoughts which **cause** out-of-control feelings (anxiety, fear, self-loathing, panic, hopelessness). Alcoholic family members, as a result of these **damaged feelings,** become estranged from themselves and those significant to them.

Recovering individuals must develop an expanded repetoire of constructive responses to stress; they can choose better to say how they feel, rather than stuff it, walk away, blame, defocus, fantasize, argue and manipulate. This requires a new perception of oneself and one's relationship to others. One can choose better not to be controlled, but to take responsibility for feelings and behavior. A clear thinking client can determine what is self-interested behavior as opposed to selfish or selfless behavior.

For the treatment community, the benefits of an alert, mentally balanced client are enormous. Such clients would be insured of energy, initiative, motivation, lack of fatigue and the ability to remain in the present while they separate out the impact the alcoholism has had on their lives, accept the reality of their situation, identify their options, use the tools and retain the content of therapy sessions and meaningful encounters with their supportive groups, readings and spiritual and social contacts. Improved intellectual capacity would mean better establishing, holding onto the integration of connections made in new learning. It would mean improved ability to screen out what is real and true for them in the present, and practice the control over their thoughts to insure that negative flashbacks do not trigger self-destructive thoughts and painful feelings. Alert clients can maintain a focus on themselves and inhibit the drifting or fogging of thought processes as painful, but necessary, material is approached in treatment. Thus, they can experience anew the distinct healing relationship between client and practitioner and use that relationship to grow.

What is Optimum Nutrition?

What is thought by many to be optimum nutrition is often not even adequate. Bacon, eggs, toast and orange juice for breakfast, a ham and cheese sandwich for lunch, roast beef, potatoes and string beans for dinner is not necessarily good nutrition. It may, in fact, be a diet that is counterproductive to recovery. Good nutrition is not eating "three squares" or popping a few vitamin pills. It is the total integration of wholesome foods and supplements into one's lifestyle and the recognition that foods typically consumed are counterproductive to proper brain function, and therefore to proper recovery.

There are many approaches to evaluating whether one's diet will produce better health or more sickness. These approaches differ, depending on how one conceptualizes the disease process. When addiction and behavioral disorders are involved, orothodox Western approaches to diet and nutrition tend to be **especially** simplistic and ineffective. Thus, it is especially important to seek alternative understandings of the meaning of optimum nutrition.

Evidence of the ineffectiveness of established dietary practices is found in meals served in most hospitals, nursing homes, schools and treatment facilities. Such meals include large amounts of sugar, caffeine, white flour and other highly processed, lifeless foods. Popular ideas regarding nutrition and behavior are limited. In the orthodox Western system, nutritional deficiency is determined largely by: (1) the appearance of acute **physical** symptoms; (2) comparing nutritional intake or blood serum levels of nutrients with the Recommended Dietary Allowance (RDA). However, nutritional deficiencies are manifested by emotional and psychological symptoms long before physical signs appear.

Whole Food for the Whole Family

Nutrition that is optimal for recovery must include at least the following features:

- A diet to control hypoglycemia or unstable blood sugar;
- Identification and removal of foods to which one is allergic, addicted, or hypersensitive;
- Moderate to large doses of certain vitamins and other therapeutic supplements to restore metabolic and nutritional balance;
- A diet consisting largely of whole unprocessed foods;
- A centered diet with minimum consumption of extreme foods;
- A plan for integrating this regimen into one's daily routine.

Hypoglycemia is a substantial risk factor in addiction and psychological disorders. Dietary control is the only generally feasible treatment and must include a diet high in complex carbohyrates and fiber, with little or no sugar, caffeine or processed carbohydrates such as white flour and white rice. Practitioners in the field of Clinical Ecology believe strongly that chemical dependency and many behavioral disorders are aggravated or sustained by foods to which one is allergic or addicted—especially foods such as wheat, corn, or yeast from which alcoholic beverages are commonly made.

A substantial amount of evidence is accumulating to indicate that many individuals who are at risk for addiction or psychological disturbances require up to 100 or even 1,000 times the amount of certain vitamins established in the RDA. In addition, a more comprehensive model for evaluating food is based not only on its nutriet content, but on the extent to which it is whole, unprocessed, and vital. An essential part of this model is based on the idea that extreme foods produce extremes in thinking and behavior, while "centered" foods produce more balanced thinking and behavior.

An extreme and uncentered diet is one that will promote addiction and behavioral disorders. It consists, on the one extreme, of large amounts of meat, eggs, salty snacks, dairy foods and highly cooked vegetables; on the other extreme are coffee, tea, soft drinks, alcohol, juices and sweet snacks. A centered diet consists primarily of whole grains, vegetables, legumes, nuts and seeds with smaller amounts of food on either extreme. A centered diet also will reduce one's craving for extreme foods. The standard American diet (SAD) consists of up to 80% of foods from either extreme. For a wide range of health reasons, Americans could profitably reverse this pattern to a diet of up to 80% of centered foods. Many families, as well as residential institutions are developing menus and eating patterns based on this approach and finding them to be cost effective as well as health and recovery effective.

What is a Healthy Family?

A healthy family is not one without problems, but one in which problems and solutions are shared, communicated and not scape-goated. A healthy family system is one in which all the members work together to nuture one another to his or her fullest potential. A healthy family allows the uniqueness of each person and respects the opinions of the feelings of its members. All members, both children and adults, are valued and given attention and access to explanations in matters of concern to them.

Adults in a healthy family role-model the values they espouse; open and concerned communication exists. People are encouraged to say how they feel and think and to take responsibility for their own actions. Activities are planned that include all members, and activities unique to each individual are encouraged. Each family member, including the very young, is included and given a contributing, belonging role in the family as a whole through chore assignments, airtime and input into decisions that affect them. There is a clear sense of individual and family identity, knowing what will happen next, and daily practice of social and communication exchanges that are enhancing to the development of self-esteem. The integration of wellness-promoting habits into the family routine can be an important part of the scenario. Wholesome food can be an important step toward the nutritional and social integrity of the family.

Family Intervention: The Calm Before the Storm

By Mary Bratton, M.S., C.A.C.

It is understandable that we, as counselors, place the major emphasis in intervention training on the event itself, on that overwhelming moment the chemically dependent person enters a roomful of people from his family, and we begin the confrontation that will hopefully culminate in a commitment to treatment. Yet that session has little chance of real success if our focus has not been primarily on the process that has gone before—our intervention with the family itself, the intervention before the intervention.

The emotional reality of a family approaching intervention must be first affirmed and then altered. As the behavior of the chemically dependent person has become more inconsistent and more unpredictable over the years, families have become locked more and more tightly into denial, repression and distrust. Their rules of communication are three: Don't talk, don't feel, and don't trust. In a misguided effort to protect both the chemically dependent person and other members of the family from pain, they fail to talk to each other about the increasingly distressful behavior created by the disease; they learn to cover up their agonizing feelings of anger and hurt and betrayal; they experience a growing distrust of all human relationships as they become unable to trust one of the most important people in their lives. We now ask that they talk to a counselor and to each other about their feelings with trust, an all but impossible task for them. Intervention training that is not sensitive to these primal facts of the family's existence is probably doomed to fail.

It is not enough to assume that the family knows there is a problem and is ready to proceed with intervention simply because they have presented themselves for training. They have come out of desperation and helplessness, and it is very rare to find more than one or two people in the entire family group more than minimally convinced that the intervention is truly necessary or possible. In fact, most family members are so reluctant to break from this position of hopelessness that I ask the person who initially contacts me to approach significant others, not with the idea of intervention, but rather with a request to "come talk to a counselor just once to see if there is some way we as a family can help." It is up to us as counselors to sell the family on intervention and on their own power.

This begins with education. It is critical that the family understand that dependency is a real disease with signs and symptoms, progression, and a fatal outcome if untreated. This involves more than just a lip service approach to the idea of the disease; we must share research and knowledge, albeit on a basic level, to give the disease meat and bones for them. We must move them from denial to a conviction that there is a problem, move them to the belief that "this is a sick person who needs to get well, rather than a bad person who needs to get good." They must also come to understand that the chemically dependent person is not deliberately deceiving them. They must know how the chemical itself prevents him from seeing his own problem. Despite their assertion that "he should know all this," the chemically dependent person is, in fact, denying a part of reality, seeing another part of reality through drug-distorted eyes, and forgetting the rest of reality in blackouts.

It is then necessary to role-model open, honest, non-judgmental communication about the disease and the feelings it engenders to help the family break the conspiracy of silence in which they have all been existing. This means a great deal of the work done in the early stages of intervention training must be done by the counselor. As family members begin to communicate honestly with each other, first about what has been happening, and then about how that has affected each of them, their initial amazement about how much each has covered up and how much each of them knew but did not reveal, gives way to a new level of sharing, affection, and bonding. They begin to support and help one another, and the family moves from a closed and defeated position, to an incredibly solid commitment to getting help for the chemically dependent person; they grow past anger and guilt to love and caring. It is then, and only then, that real intervention training can begin.

At this point, the intervention counselor must become a member of the family and guide the family gently beyond their fear and apprehension and skepticism to see and feel the combined power of the intervention team. The family has facts about the illness, and what has been happening; the counselor has the possibility and mechanism of recovery to offer. Together we will break the pattern of earlier confrontations, change all the previous rules, and open the door for treatment and recovery.

In the past, the chemically dependent person has likely been approached by one person, around one or two provoking incidents, with angry accusations, and with an open-ended demand that "things must change." Sometimes there has even been an admission of a problem as a result of such an encounter, leading only to more intense feelings of confusion and inadequacy when the using continues unabated. Now we will approach the chemically dependent person together, with love and care and concern, paint a picture for him with facts about what drugs and alcohol have been doing in his life, and offer him a way out. For this reason, it is critical that the emphasis in the fact lists be placed on "the good person you are and can be," even as we demonstrate how the drugs are pulling that good person away from himself and us. It is much more important that the chemically dependent person hear how chemicals are isolating him from the people who care for him than any litany of offenses committed under the influence; it is much more imporant for him to hear how depressed and lonely he appears than how bad he has been; it is much more important for him to hear how good they believe it can be than how awful it as been. The chemically dependent person is prepared for anger and has defenses to deal with that; he is not prepared for concern and care and has no human defenses against love. I am convinced that the facts shared in an intervention are much less important than the love and hope expressed. We will literally punch through the face of that wall of defenses around the chemically dependent person, but more importantly, we will be there, holding hands in love, to catch him when he falls. I am also convinced that a recovering person must be involved in the intervention itself, either as counselor or another member of the team, so that the chemically dependent person can freely identify with the illness and the possibility of recovery at that vulnerable point.

It is rarely that we can scare anyone into treatment. We want more than that. We want the chemically dependent person to make the decision to get help, not because he is being forced to, but because his family's love and concern convince him that he can love himself, and that he is worth recovery. We do not want to spend valuable treatment time rebuilding a devastated ego; we want the patient free to express genuine gratitude and love to this family, if not in the intervention itself, then shortly afterwards. We want the family to feel strong and loving, not an antagonistic "gang." For this reason, I am reluctant to use consequences in an intervention, and I have used them only to secure an agreement for immediate admission, once the decision for treatment has been reached. If love fails, threats will likely not succeed.

Because we are putting the chemically dependent person directly into treatment from the intervention, both to prevent his defenses from re-emerging and to provide closure and alleviate stress for the family, it is imperative that the admitting staff be made peripheral members of the intervention team. As well as dealing with symptoms of physical stress, e.g., elevated blood pressure, they will need to provide support for emotional stress with T.L.C. and reinforcement of the family's love and the patient's courage in opting for treatment. This, too, will pave the way for gratitude.

Of course, a successful intervention must be orchestrated, from writing fact lists to the final role play, from booking a bed to clearing away all possible objections to immediate admission. However, the most alteration and growth wrought in the family's communication and affect, and no amount of mechanical preparation can substitute for that emotional metamorphosis. I am convinced that no intervention ever fails, if we bear in mind that our primary goal is to change the family. Treatment follows as the logical consequence of that change.

Alcohol's Effects on Pregnancy, Birth, and Growth: FAE/FAS

By Eileen M. Ouelette, M.D.

Presented to the House Select Committee on Children, Youth & Families—June 30, 1983

Definition

Fetal Alcohol Syndrome (FAS) refers to a series of effects seen in children of women who chronically drink alcohol to excess during, and possibly prior to, pregnancy. Minimum criteria for the diagnosis of FAS are:

1. Prenatal and/or postnatal growth retardation, with weight, length, and/or head circumference below the tenth percentile.
2. Central nervous sytem involvement, with neurologic abnormality, developmental delay or intellectual impairment.
3. Facial dysmorphology (birth defects) with at least 2/3 signs:
   a. microcephaly (small brain);
   b. microphthalmia (small eyes) and/or short palpebral fissures (the horizontal length of the eyes);
   c. poorly developed philtrum (the distance from the base of the nose to the upper lip), thin upper lip, and/or flattening of the maxillary area.

The spectrum of clinical features currently known is shown in Table 1.

Fetal Alcohol Effects (FAE) refers to any abnormalities seen in children as a result of alcohol use by women during pregnancy.

GROWTH ABNORMALITIES
1. Premature birth
2. Prenatal growth retardation
3. Postnatal growth retardation
   a. short stature
   b. diminished weight

SKULL & FACIAL DEFORMITIES
1. Small head compared to rest of body (associated with mental retardation)
2. Eye abnormalities
   a. oriental-looking eyes
   b. Shortened horizontal eye length
   c. corneal opacity
   d. drooping eyelids
   e. pronounced nearsightedness
   f. squinting
   g. twisted blood vessels in the retina
   h. eyes appear widespaced but are not
3. Flattened nasal bridge
4. Abnormally formed ears
5. Defective development of tissue in jaw
6. Thin upper lip
7. Small lower jaw
8. Cleft palate

JOINT & LIMB MALFORMATIONS
1. Limitation of elbow extension
2. Toe & finger irregularities
   a. small nails
   b. permanently bent fingers
3. Dislocated hips
4. Abnormal creases in the palm of hand

CARDIAC ABNORMALITIES
1. Defects in the wall between the atria
2. Defects in the lower chamber of heart
3. Narrowing of the pulmonary artery, enlargement of the right ventricle, misplaced aorta, defects in the wall between the ventricles.
4. Persistence of an opening between the main pulmonary artery and the aorta
5. Interruption of the curved part of aorta
6. Narrowing of the opening into the pulmonary artery from the right cardiac ventricle.

KIDNEY IRREGULARITIES
1. Single kidney
2. Collection of urine in the kidney pelvis due to obstructed outflow
3. Defective development of kidneys

FUNCTIONAL ABNORMALITIES

Neonatal
1. Poor sucking ability
2. Loss of muscle tone
3. Trembling or shaking

Postnatal
1. Delayed development
2. Mental retardation
3. Poor gross motor coordination
4. Poor fine motor coordination
5. Learning disabilities
6. Hyperactivity
7. Decreased attention span

OTHER FINDINGS
1. Accumulation of cerebrospinal fluid within brain ventricles
2. Neural tube defects in fetus
3. Single umbilical artery
4. Noonan syndrome
5. Klippel-Feil syndrome (short & wide neck, low hairline, reduction in number of cervical vertibrae, fusion of cervical spine, etc.)
6. Accessory nipples
7. Abnormal external genitalia
8. Benign tumors of capillaries
9. Spastic stiffness of the limbs
10. Cancer of the adrenal gland

Frequency

There were 3,704,000 babies born in the United States in 1982. FAS is estimated to occur between 1 and 2 per thousand live births for the full constellation of features (3,700 to 7,400 babies), with the frequency of partial expression at possibly between 3 to 5 per thousand live births (11,100 to 18,500 babies). It is the third most common cause of mental retardation and is more common than Down's syndrome. FAS is totally preventable!

Information is still lacking concerning the full scope and gravity of the ill effects on the fetus and infant of chronic maternal alcohol abuse prior to and during pregnancy. Effects produced range from mildly impaired to profoundly afflicted children, and some fatalities have been reported. It is unknown how many children's lives have been premanently afflicted by excessive alcohol use in their mothers. The risk of producing an abnormal child for a mother with alcohol abuse is unknown. Some evidence exists that children are more at risk for abnormalities with each successive pregnancy in which the mother continues to drink heavily.

The majority of children show only some of the abnormalities described. Alcohol embryopathy should be suspected when growth retardation and/or congenital anomalies are present in a child and a careful history of ethanol abuse should be elicted from the mother. Unfortunately, there are no laboratory tests which are diagnostic of this disorder, nor is there any present capability of identifying abnormal fetuses by amniocentesis.

Moderate Alcohol Use

Studies on moderate drinking during pregnancy, equivalent to a daily consumption of 2 oz. of 100-proof whiskey, is associated with lower birth weight in offspring and increased prematurity rates. Concurrent use of marijuana while pregnancy may increase the risk of developing FAS.

Safe levels of alcohol intake during pregnancy, if any, have yet to be determined. At the present time, we recommend that pregnant women abstain from alcohol, but advise women that an occasional alcoholic beverage has not been found to be harmful to the fetus. Similar recommendations are made to nursing mothers.

Maternal/Child Effects of Alcohol

Alcohol passes rapidly from the maternal circulation to the fetus and assumes approximately the same concentration as in maternal blood. Alcohol levels within the fetal circulation fall more slowly than in the maternal circulation, so that detctable levels of alcohol are still present in the fetus after the alcohol has been totally cleared from the maternal circulation. Not only does alcohol enter the fetal circulation, but it is excreted into the amniotic fluid where it remains in essentially the same concentration for several hours until slowly being cleared. Changes are seen in fetal acid-base balance, cerebral function and metabolism. Alcohol has also been found to reach human milk in a similar concentration to that in peripheral maternal blood, decreasing together with decreasing ethanol content of the blood.

Women and Alcohol

The National Institute on Alcohol Abuse and Alcoholism (NIAAA) reports that in 1950 one in every eight alcoholics was a woman. In 1982, one in every three alcoholics was a woman. Excessive drinking is rising at a rapid rate. The highest proportion of heavy drinkers among women is between the ages of 21-29, the age of peak reproductive years. The second highest is in the teenage years. Current NIAAA statistics report that there are 2.25 million women problem drinkers and 3 million teen problem drinkers in the United States.

The use of alcohol among girls and among women is approaching that of boys and men. Reliable data concerning alcoholism in women are difficult to come by, as the female alcoholic has a greater tendency to drink secretly in the privacy of her home and therefore comes to professional attention later than the male alcoholic, who often is identified through poor work performance or automobile accidents.

Recent studies show that all women tend to decrease their alcohol intake during the early months of pregnancy, presumably from a combination of factors.

Prevention Strategies

Child-oriented. It must be stressed again that the Fetal Alcohol Syndrome and its spectrum of abnormalities are a totally preventable cause of growth abnormalities, congenital malformations and mental retardation. Intense and extensive preventive strategies should be undertaken, as there is no known way to reverse or reduce the effects of alcohol on the fetus once they have occurred. Once a baby has been born with signs of FAS, early identification of the problem, treatment for specific clinical findings, infant stimulation and close attention to nutritional problems are vital.

In our experience, much of the post-natal growth retardation seen in these children is due to their active rejection of food. Videotapes which we have made indicate that the children have increased but uncoordinated sucking and swallowing movements, coupled with extrusion movements of the tongue, so that their intake of food is less than adequate and feeding times are prolonged. Even highly experienced foster mothers find these children extremely difficult to feed. Generally, feeding problems are significant for the first year of life and gradually improve so that by the time the children are 3 to 4 years of age, they are consuming a more adequate diet, although they continue to be highly selective in their food preferences.

Pregnant Women and Mothers. Two sites are especially useful in the identification of women of child-bearing age who have alcohol-related problems. Family planning and prenatal clinics are ideal locations for educational programs and places where women with alcohol problems should be identified.

Questions about alcohol use should be routinely asked of women at the first prenatal visit. A brief questionnaire developed by Rosett et al. has been found to be useful in identifying moderate and havy drinkers in a non-threatening and non-time consuming manner.

Table II. Ten Question Drinking History for Prenatal Use

Beer: How many times per week? _____
How many cans each time? _____
Ever drink more?

Wine: How many times per week? _____
How many glasses each time? _____
Ever drink more?

Liquor: How many times per week? _____
How many drinks each time? _____
Ever drink more?

Has your drinking changed in the last year?

We and others have found that the prenatal clinic is an ideal site for initiating intervention in women previously unidentified as having alcohol-related problems. Women so identified should be referred to alcohol treatment centers for additional counseling and support. The women are generally highly motivated to alter their drinking behavior in order to produce offspring with the least possible risk. Their repeated associations over several months with health care deliveries assist them to form therapeutic relationships. Heavy drinking women who stop drinking during pregnancy have a good chance of delivering a normal child. Although no improvement in the risk of congenital malformations could be expected due to their appearance early in the pregnancy, the risk of prematurity and growth retardation is lessened.

In the postnatal period, there is an increased risk of recidivism. The impetus for modifying behavior is often less after the baby has been born. The increased stress of taking care of an infant may cause the mother to revert to previous drinking patterns, particularly if the infant has problems, such as poor feeding, sleeping, and restlessness.

The importance of outreach efforts and home visits during this period cannot be overemphasized. Women often find it more difficult to keep appointments outside the home in the postnatal period, but welcome visits by a therapeutic nurse practitioner, alcoholism counselor or other therapist. Women should have a telephone number to call 24 hours a day in case significant problems arise. Referral to strong supportive programs, such as Alcoholics Anonymous, are important throughout the prenatal and postnatal periods.

Education Programs. The Eunice Kennedy Shriver Center for Mental Retardation in Waltham, Massachusetts, has been designated as a New England Regional resource for the prevention and treatment of the Fetal Alcohol Syndrome. We have developed a variety of educational programs for health care and other professionals, alcohol treament centers, families, including foster parents, teachers, junior high, high school, and college students, and the public at large. The goal of these programs is to identify and refer women at risk. It is extremely important that practicing physicians and house officers in the field of obstetrics and gynecology, family practice and pediatrics be aware of the harmful effects of maternal alcohol abuse on offpsring, that they seek and recognize those at risk, that they become skilled in ascertaining drinking histories, and that they have knowledge of local resources to refer people for assistance. Scientific presentations, publication of articles in professional journals, and participation in hospital departmental grand rounds are all useful means of providing this type of education.

Nurses, particularly those employed in prenatal clinics and newborn nurseries, midwives, staffs of family planning agencies, social workers, psychologists, alcoholism counselors and teachers are frequently the first to identify families with alcohol-related problems. Participation in workshops, health fairs, and in-service training sessions has been very effective in new case findings.

Families themselves, including foster families and mothers in alcohol treatment centers and halfway houses benefit not only from individual therapy, but gain knowledge and skills from being given factual information in a group setting. This format increases their understanding and recognition of common problems and assists them to ask questions of their individual physicians and other therapists.

It should be stressed that women in halfway houses comprise a special audience. They are often in different stages of recovery and guilt. Prior staff preparation and presentation of child-related information in a non-threatening and supportive fashion is essential. In some cases, it is wiser for individuals to defer participation in some of the FAS educational programs until they themnselves are further along in their recovery.

Another important part of our educational program is our participation in school health curricula. Our FAS program director has prepared an educational package consisting of a slide tape, verbal presentation and question and answer session, which is now part of the Health Care Curriculum in a number of local schools.

A special program has been developed for pregnant teenagers, who continue to attend high school. The focus is on the use and abuse of alcohol as part of general health issues. A list of common nonprescription medications containing alcohol is provided to them to make them realize the need to be aware of the contents of everything they ingest while pregnant.

A final form of educational program is that of increasing public awareness. Public service announcements of 30 seconds each are routinely aired on local and regional TV stations. Brochures have been developed for placement in physicians offices, family planning agencies, prenatal clinics, libraries, schools, churches, alcohol treatment agencies, women's groups and treatment centers. Others have utilized marriage license bureaus and diaper services to educate the general public about FAS.

Summary

The re-identification of the risk of maternal alcohol use during pregnancy jand the recognition of the effects of alcohol on fetal development are only ten years old. Much remains to be learned about the cause and scope of the problem. Unlike genetic disorders, it is totally preventable. Early identification of those at risk and increased public awareness continue to be our best weapons in combatting this important public health program.

Books About Families & Chemical Dependency

...also available from Health Communications, Inc.

- **Changing Legacies: Growing Up in An Alcoholic Home** **$6.95**
  Code No. 22H99 (Soft Cover)
- **Co-Dependency: An Emerging Issue** **$6.95**
  Code No. 22H101 (Soft Cover)

- **Another Chance: Hope & Health for Alcoholic Families** (Sharon Wegscheider-Cruse) **$14.95**
- **It Will Never Happen to Me** (Claudia Black) **$7.95**
  Code No. 40H92 (Soft Cover)
- **Marriage on the Rocks** (Janet Woititz) **$6.95**
  Code No. 22H96 (Soft Cover)
- **The Family Therapy of Drug Abuse and Addiction** (Duncan Stanton & Thomas Todd, Eds.) **$25.95**
  Code No. 40H91 (Hard Cover)
- **Adult Children of Alcoholics** (Janet Woititz) **$5.95**
  Code No. 22H95 (Soft Cover)

TO ORDER:

1. List requested titles on a separate sheet of paper.
2. Add total price of books.
3. Orders over $20.00 can be billed to a Purchase Order or credit card (MasterCard or VISA).
4. Orders under $20.00 must be prepaid.
5. Shipping and Handling:
   Minimum — $1.25 for orders less than $25.00.
   5% of total for orders over $25.00.

Mail Your Order To:

Health Communications, Inc.
2119-A Hollywood Blvd.
Hollywood, FL 33020
Phone Orders—(305) 920-9435 — Please have Purchase Order Number or Credit Card ready. Thank You.